Comprehensive Crisis Intervention Manual

Crisis Intervention for School and Community Personnel

- *Immediate Response Checklists* included to guide immediate responses
  during a crisis.

- Strategies and activities for dealing with students, adults, crisis-team staff, as well as business and community members.

- Interventions addressing a comprehensive range of crises including accidents, sudden loss, suicide, violence and large-scale disasters.

- Numerous checklists and specialized forms to help organize and manage a school-based or community response team during a crisis.

Peter F. White, M.A. - Edited by David W. Peat, Ph.D.

Inquiries concerning crisis intervention training workshops, please contact:

Peter F. White   Dr. David W. Peat

E-mail: defacto2@gmail.com   peatandassociates@gmail.com

The writer and editor would appreciate any information, suggestions, or constructive comments that may improve future editions of this manual.

Order this book online at www.trafford.com/07-3044
or email orders@trafford.com

Most Trafford titles are also available at major online book retailers.

Note for Librarians: A cataloguing record for this book is available from Library and Archives Canada at www.collectionscanada.ca/amicus/index-e.html

Printed in Victoria, BC, Canada.

ISBN: 978-1-4251-6579-6

We at Trafford believe that it is the responsibility of us all, as both individuals and corporations, to make choices that are environmentally and socially sound. You, in turn, are supporting this responsible conduct each time you purchase a Trafford book, or make use of our publishing services. To find out how you are helping, please visit www.trafford.com/responsiblepublishing.html

Our mission is to efficiently provide the world's finest, most comprehensive book publishing service, enabling every author to experience success. To find out how to publish your book, your way, and have it available worldwide, visit us online at www.trafford.com/10510

 **www.trafford.com**

North America & international
toll-free: 1 888 232 4444 (USA & Canada)
phone: 250 383 6864 ♦ fax: 250 383 6804 ♦ email: info@trafford.com

The United Kingdom & Europe
phone: +44 (0)1865 722 113 ♦ local rate: 0845 230 9601
facsimile: +44 (0)1865 722 868 ♦ email: info.uk@trafford.com

10 9 8 7 6 5 4 3 2

Peter White and David Peat first met in the 1990's while they were colleague psychologists in the Yukon Territory, Canada. They periodically kept in touch, and finally were able to work together again in Singapore and the Maldives during 2005. They continue to collaborate in various ways, in spite of living in different parts of Canada.

PETER WHITE

Peter White is from Nova Scotia, Canada and moved from Halifax to Whitehorse, Yukon Territory, Canada in 1991. He has been employed with the Yukon Territory Government's Department of Education Special Programs Branch as an Educational Psychologist since that time. Peter completed his Bachelor of Arts degree in Logic and Semantics at Dalhousie University in Halifax, his Bachelor of Education degree at Acadia University in Wolfville, and his Master of Arts degree in Educational Psychology and Measurement at Mount Saint Vincent University in Halifax. Prior to relocating to Whitehorse, Peter worked as an Educational Psychologist with the Nova Scotia Hospital's Psychology Department in Dartmouth, as a Training Officer with the Nova Scotia Hospital's Staff Development Department, and as an Educational Psychologist with the Terra Nova and Cape Freels Integrated School Boards in Newfoundland. Peter has also worked as an Educational Psychologist with the Sooke District School Board on Vancouver Island, the Prince George District School Board in central British Columbia, and as a 'free-lance' psychologist in Atlin, northern British Columbia. Recently, Peter worked in Singapore with Peat & Associates as an Educational Psychologist conducting assessments and presenting teacher in-services at international schools. He also assisted in the delivery of post-tsunami, trainer-of-trainer workshops for Community-level Workers in Male, Republic of Maldives.

Peter has a keen interest in test construction, research design, measurement and program evaluation. While working with the Nova Scotia Hospital, he designed and developed the *White-Woods Performance Checklist*, and accompanying training video. This instrument was designed to evaluate one and two-person Cardio-pulmonary resuscitation procedures. In addition, he developed, in consultation with the hospital programmer, a computer-based *Patient Tracking System* used by one hospital unit and a number of *Checklists for Survey Research at the Nova Scotia Hospital*. As a trainer and consultant for the Federal Government of Canada, Peter designed a number of *Performance Appraisal Instruments (BOS and BARS)* to evaluate field-training competence at the individual and group level and he also conducted peer reviews.

From 1980 to 1987, Peter was the chief rock-climbing instructor for the Canadian Hostelling Association in Halifax, where he taught rock climbing schools and clinics. He has also taught specialized cliff rescues courses to Parks Canada wardens in Nova Scotia and Newfoundland, as well as provincial park wardens and fire departments. Peter continues to be involved in rock and ice climbing, cross-country skiing, and mountain biking.

DAVID PEAT

Dr. Peat has been involved in the fields of education, rehabilitation and health in various capacities since 1972. As a public and private school teacher, Dr. Peat has instructed people of all ages, most frequently those with 'special needs'. Responsibilities within school settings have included being a science, mathematics and physical education teacher, a 'special education' teacher, a psychologist, a school administrator, a district-level coordinator of 'special services' and an associate superintendent of schools.

In 1984, he took a leave from teaching and administration to obtain Masters of Education and Ph.D. degrees. During this time he also earned an Intercultural Certificate, qualified as a reading clinician and was registered as a psychologist (College of Alberta Psychologists, Canada). As a psychologist, Dr. Peat worked in various settings in Canada, including the remote Northern Arctic territory of Yukon. Internationally, he was employment in Kuwait, Qatar and Singapore in hospital, private school and government settings. His work emphasized the thorough assessment of abilities in order to develop appropriate educational, medical and community-based plans and interventions. Within Education Ministries and School Boards in Canada, Dr. Peat has been a Coordinator of Special Education Services, Curriculum Evaluator and Associate Superintendent of Schools. He has also served as a consultant, helping schools to develop programs and interventions for students with behavioural difficulties; designing and implementing locally developed 'thinking-skills' programs; and evaluating special education services.

Working with both experienced and prospective teachers has been a major thrust for Dr. Peat. At the university and college level, he has taught courses entitled *Problems of Attention and Behaviour, Nature and Characteristics of Learning Disabilities, Educational Procedures for the Learning Disabled, Overview of 'Exceptionalities'*, and *The Diverse Classroom: Curriculum Adaptations and Modifications*. Presentations and seminars to schools, teachers and community agencies in Canada, Kuwait, Qatar and Singapore have been on topics such as *The Direct Instruction of Thinking Skills to Students, Student Assessment, Curriculum Evaluation, Child Development, Parenting, Discipline, Strategic Planning, Stress, Grief and Loss, Post Traumatic Stress Disorder, Critical Incident Stress Defusing* and *How to Design Presentations based upon Adult Learning Principles,* to name a few.

Research, coupled with publications in books and journals, has spanned the topics of literacy, the teaching of thinking skills, curriculum development, instructional practices, change theory, staff development, topics of health & wellness and assessment models/instruments. He is a co-author of a 'thinking skills' program entitled *SPELT (Strategy Programme for Effective Learning and Thinking)*, which has been implemented with students and teachers in Canada, Korea, India, Australia, New Zealand and other parts of the world.

From 1997 until 2005, Dr. Peat worked internationally as a psychologist in the Arabian Gulf with the *Kuwait-Dalhousie Physiotherapy and Rehabilitation Project, The Learning Centre* in Doha, Qatar and in Singapore. In Kuwait his responsibilities included consulting with clinical specialty rehabilitation teams in a hospital setting spanning the areas of neurology, orthopaedics, paediatrics, burns and cardiovascular rehabilitation. Direct patient treatment and family consultations addressed issues such as stress, anxiety, depression, anger management, moving towards the acceptance of disabling conditions, coping with grief and loss and behavioural issues. Facilitating the development of smooth patient transitions from hospital-based to school and community-based services was a strong focus of his work. Collaborating with a Health Educator, Carolyn Madden and clinical teams, they developed and implemented clinical, educational and preventative programs aimed at helping Kuwait citizens lower their risk of disease and/or injury and to adopt more healthy lifestyles (e.g., Smoking Cessation; Stress Management).

In the educational setting of *The Learning Centre* in Qatar, Dr. Peat, as Deputy Head & Psychologist, was responsible for the oversight, development and implementation of individual educational plans (IEPs) for children with special needs. He also provided advice to administrators and committees concerning service delivery models and systemic approaches to solving school-based issues (e.g., bullying). On an individual client basis, he provided psycho-educational assessments for children suspected of having learning disabilities or developmental disabilities; provided counselling services to children and their families; consulted with parents, 'regular education' school staff and other professionals; and conducted in-service education workshops for parents and teachers.

Dr. Peat resided in Singapore from 2000-2006 initially working as a Senior Educational Psychologist for the Ministry of Education. For his first year in Singapore his responsibilities encompassed the development and/or adaptation of *Singapore-based and normed* assessment instruments in areas such as talent & ability identification, mathematical abilities and cognitive development and being a consultant to Gifted Education Program specialists. The following two years he provided psychological services to schools, delivered professional development sessions to teachers, parents and administrators concerning theory and instructional methods for those with learning difficulties (e.g., dyslexia, autism, intellectual disabilities, etc.) and gave advice to policy makers. From 2004-2006, he was employed with the Child Guidance Clinic, Institute of Mental Health, Singapore as a Senior Educational Psychologist responsible for establishing and guiding the COPES (Children's One-stop Psycho-educational Services) Programme. In addition, he was the Academic Director (Education) for James Cook University, Singapore.

Presently, Dr. Peat is the Associate Superintendent of Learning with the Rocky View School Division #41, Airdrie, Alberta, Canada. His responsibilities include overseeing four Branches within the Learning Department, specifically, Student Support, Collaborative Initiatives, Instructional Support and Technology.

During his time when not engaged with the above position, he is engaged as a 'free-lance' psychologist, consultant, lecturer and curriculum|technology developer. His work emphasizes the translation of psychological, instructional and developmental theory to intervention and practice. Consulting and teaching in the Maldives, Philippines and Sri Lanka, specifically on the topics of post-disaster psychosocial support and the development of integrated support services for *all* children, was, and continues to be, a passion.

PREFACE

Developing a workable and meaningful school and/or community crisis plan is not simply a task for large urban schools. There is a need for *all* schools and communities to have such a plan in place. Increasingly schools have to cope with student fights, weapons in the school, drug abuse, gangs, and other forms of violent behaviors that are not exclusive to the larger city schools. Schools mirror the wider society; therefore much of the information contained in this manual also applies to communities. Although it is not possible to completely protect children or a school from these issues, a comprehensive and collaboratively developed crisis plan can go a long way to reduce the adverse effects that these kinds of traumatic events can have on the lives of children. It has been consistently proven that prior crisis planning can make a significant difference in an emergency situation. When a comprehensive strategy is in place, it allows school staff to more effectively and responsibly protect children and lessen the impact of a traumatic event.

Recent history has shown us that advance planning for large-scale disasters due to natural causes such as hurricanes, cyclones, floods, tsunamis or man-made catastrophic events, also needs to be undertaken.

The author would like to express sincere thanks and appreciation to all the teachers, principals, school staff, and community agencies that provided numerous suggestions after having been involved in one crisis or another.

I would especially thank Leona Zinn for her strong support and encouragement, without which this manual would not have been completed. I would particularly like to thank a true expert in the field of critical incident intervention and friend, Althea Woods, for her invaluable input and guidance drafting this manual. As well, I would like to thank Dr. Robert McClelland and Patricia McClelland for their excellent initial editing and advice and Stephen White for his invaluable proof reading. This training manual was developed from involvement in specific workshops and clinics on crisis intervention and suicide prevention coupled with extensive first-hand experience responding to numerous crises and traumatic events in both urban and rural schools located in the Yukon Territory of Canada.

Thank you from both Peter White and Dr. David Peat to the people of Maldives for their contribution to the development of portions of this manual during a training-of-trainers workshop following the tragic tsunami of 2004. We salute the resilience and kindness of the people of the Maldives, particularly the staff and directors of *The Care Society*, Male'. As well, *ActionAid's* funding for the workshop and the on-going post-tsunami support for Maldivians and other vulnerable peoples of the world is greatly esteemed.

Note:

A training manual has been produced from the original *Comprehensive Critical Incident Intervention* manual for the Care Society, Republic of Maldives. This training manual was collaboratively developed and contextualized by community care workers and other professionals working with victims of the Tsunami, including displaced families and individuals.

The model used to train community-based workers in the Maldives is envisioned to be further expanded into a comprehensive 'Trainer of Trainers' manual, designed to accompany this *Comprehensive Crisis Intervention Manual*. It will provide detailed information about **Learner Centered** and **Leader Centered** activities as well as numerous activities for both, and will be available during 2008.

TABLE OF CONTENTS

PART 6.   GUIDELINES FOR CRISIS DEBRIEFING   71

PART 7.   THE MEMORIAL SERVICE   83

PART 8.   THE AFTERMATH   87

PART 9.   RESPONSE TO SPECIFIC CRISES   95

PART 10.   DEVELOPING A COMPREHENSIVE CRISIS PLAN   117

PART 1. INTRODUCTION

HOW TO USE THIS MANUAL

This manual has been divided into sections according to specific areas of crisis and their related suggested interventions. **Part 1, Introduction** provides the rationale for the Manual and includes a summary of the procedures and strategies presented. **Part 2, Initial Preparation** defines a crisis and presents an outline for selecting crisis team. members and developing a school-based crisis plan. **Part 3, School/Community Crisis Team in Action** deals with the immediate response by a school crisis team, the actions that should be taken, and intervention strategies for kindergarten, elementary, and junior/senior students. **Part 4, Dealing with the Media and Parents** presents information about how school officials should respond to media attention. As well, there is information about responding to parental concerns and strategies parents can implement to help their children cope with a traumatic event. **Part 5, Crisis Counseling** consists of basic information necessary for conducting specific types of crisis counseling and ways of minimizing the short and long-term negative effects of experiencing a traumatic event. **Part 6, Guidelines for Crisis Debriefing** presents a specific model for conducting classroom debriefings. **Part 7, The Memorial Service** provides ideas concerning preparing students for a memorial service and presents suggestions for student involvement. **Part 8, The Aftermath** consists of information about vicarious trauma and guidelines for debriefing school staff, crisis response team members, and department personnel. **Part 9, Response to Specific Crises** presents information about responding to specific traumatic events. **Part 10, Developing your School's Crisis Plan** contains suggestions for developing a crisis plan that will meet the needs of your school.

Appendix 1 is a list of suggested readings and resources. **Appendix 2** contains pocket sized reference cards for each of the debriefings used as an intervention. These are described in greater detail below. **Appendix 3** contains the **Rapid Response Checklists**. These checklists can be used when responding to various crises and critical incidents or when you need to know what to do first.

CONTEXTUALIZING THE INFORMATION FOR YOUR SCHOOL OR COMMUNITY SETTING

An electronic version (MSWord) of all forms and checklists in the Appendices of this manual may be obtained by sending an email to either Peter White or Dr. David Peat (See *Copyright Page* for e-mail addresses). This service is intended to help School Administrators and Community Leaders develop a school- or community-based critical incident intervention plan. The MSWord format allows crisis team members to tailor the forms and checklists to their particular context (e.g., school, school-system or community), as part of the process of developing a workable crisis plan. In addition, by providing these forms and checklists in this way, the information can be easily changed in format (e.g., *Powerpoint*) for instructional and/or planning purposes.

Once a crisis plan has been developed and team members selected or appointed, all members should become familiar with the plan so as to ensure its smooth operation in the event of a critical incident occurring. A school or community crisis intervention plan should be considered similar to a fire drill. For the plan to work effectively, everyone on the team must know the plan well. Periodically the plan should be reviewed and practiced, with changes made where necessary. Revisions and/or reviews should be recorded on the **School/Community Incident Plan Review** form. This will demonstrate a level of quality assurance for the school or community critical incident intervention plan. The original purchaser of the manual is permitted to copy, edit and contextualize the forms on the compact disk.

POCKET REFERENCE CARDS

Specific tables in the manual have been printed in small-size format in **Appendix 2**. They are: *Defusing Emotions, Group Debriefing, Classroom Debriefing, Individual Debriefing, Operational Debriefing* and *Suicide Risk Assessment*. These sheets are designed to that they can be carried in a pocket and accessed quickly and discretely, to be used for a handy reference, as necessary.

USING THE RAPID RESPONSE CHECKLISTS

Rapid Response Checklists are located in **<u>Appendix 3</u>**. They are intended as a quick reference when a crisis occurs and you need to know the first steps. The reader can quickly determine whether an action has taken place by looking to see if it has been checked **yes** or **no**. This provides a written record as to the action taken and the individual responsible for taking the action. The first checklist titled, **IMMEDIATE RESPONSE** outlines those steps that should be followed when responding to most critical incidents. Once the reader has sufficient time he or she should read the appropriate section(s) of the manual that are pertinent to the situation at hand. The format of these forms has been adapted from a manual produced by Educational Service (1997).

PART 2. INITIAL PREPARATION

PURPOSE

A trauma shatters the foundations of trust and order expected from authority. Students assume school is a safe environment comprised of people who care about them. When so many distraught individuals are obviously being ignored, their trust in the world is even further undermined. The erratic behavior and emotional displays are difficult to contain. Control and routines are lost at a time when students need strong control coupled with deep understanding and compassion.

School staff should understand that the days following a sudden death or other traumatic event will be a time in which there is considerable confusion, with emotions running high. The levels of confusion and emotional reaction are a direct result of the traumatic event and the response by school personnel. It must be kept in mind that the aforementioned factors will have a direct effect on the type and degree of intervention taken at the school.

It is important to understand that a formal response to most crises lasts approximately three days with a follow-up scheduled within two weeks and another one at six weeks. Crises affect everyone; teachers, administration, students, secretaries, and custodial staff. The purpose of any crisis intervention is to provide students and staff with a supportive atmosphere where they can express their feelings and fears openly and safely. The long-term goal of crisis intervention is to help students and staff return to their pre-crisis level of functioning. This is achieved by helping individuals understand their reactions to the event and determine what they need to do next. Crisis intervention does not use psychotherapy or any other form of therapy; it does, however, attempt to strengthen defenses so individuals can deal with the existing and often overwhelming stress of the current situation. In addition, implementing crisis intervention procedures helps to reduce the potential effects of traumatic stress over a longer period of time.

- ### *Reducing Traumatic Stress*

Traumatic stress is an emotional crisis brought on by externally imposed stresses or situations that are unexpected, uncontrollable, and overwhelming. Individuals experiencing traumatic stress go through three stages. (**1**) Impulsive behavior, (**2**) excessive depression, and (**3**) possible psychotic breaks with anger often directed toward the school for not adequately addressing the situation. The timeliness of providing support to individuals is critical. If people are not helped to discover a balanced resolution, they are left vulnerable to disorganization. If sufficient students and staff are affected, the entire school community itself is in danger of disorganization. These effects demonstrate why an effective crisis intervention plan is so important. It is not possible to predict all crises and when they will occur; however, a flexible and previously developed crisis plan will provide the appropriate response for students and staff during a critical incident.

<u>Note</u>
According to Roberts (1990), one Junior High School experienced the death of a student who was on the periphery of the student body. Because he was relatively unknown, the school chose not to do anything to acknowledge his death. The teachers were forbidden to hold discussions with the students or comment about the incident.

Junior High Schools probably have the most effective/efficient grapevine in the world, and within hours of the incident, all the students knew. They tried to whisper among themselves and contain their reactions in the classes but this proved to be beyond their ability because of their stage of development.

For days afterward, many students were in fights. Others cried with friends and were disciplined for not being where they should have been. Some started skipping school. Three days later, the school psychologists were called to work with the students; by this time, however, the anger of the grief process had been targeted toward the school, its teachers, and principal. Many teachers were ambivalent about ignoring the death and, through their anxiety, inadvertently communicated their own discomfort to the students. Although the psychologists did work in this school for quite some time, the school never regained the allegiance and the trust of these students.

SELECTING CRISIS TEAM MEMBERS

The best crisis teams are composed of people possessing a broad perspective on life. They should have an ability to perceive multiple consequences; a willingness to challenge an idea and then work cooperatively toward a solution. The ability to think clearly under stress; flexibility; and a familiarity with the subtleties of the school, its student body, and its community are the most important attributes. Other characteristics that are desirable include a personal comfort level in discussing such issues as death and suicide. The crisis team often includes the Principal, the Vice-Principal, the school counselor, a staff member, and the secretary. Other members may be added depending upon the size of the school and the nature of the particular crisis.

- ### *Assessing Team Preparation*

All team members must be trained in crisis intervention. They must know the plan thoroughly in their own school and should be familiar with the plans at other schools where they may be expected to help. Team members must also be familiar with the strategies used for preventing Post Traumatic Stress Disorder. It is most important that all team members continuously update their skills. The following questions will help to focus on the level of preparedness of your school based crisis response team.

1. Which members lack training in individual and classroom debriefing, situational assessment, knowledge of Post Traumatic Stress Disorder, and Panic Attacks?
2. Where can this training be obtained?
3. Has a school crisis plan been previously developed?
4. If a school crisis plan has been developed, are all members familiar with the plan and their responsibilities?
5. Will the crisis team be expected to respond to all situations including violence, death, natural disasters, and other accidents?
6. Is any special equipment needed?

LEVELS OF RESPONSE TO CRISES

When a critical incident develops there will be at least two levels of response, **School Based** and **District/Division**. The **School Based** response to a crisis tends to focus on direct intervention with students and staff. The **District/Division** response to a school crisis tends to focus on indirect intervention and support to the affected school.

There are four situations when the District/Division Crisis Team or individual members may be sent directly to a school. **(1)** There is insufficient staff to make up a School-based Crisis Team at the affected school. **(2)** It is District/Division policy to dispatch crisis teams or individual members to the affected school. **(3)** The School-based Crisis Team itself is in a crisis state (this state may arise if the death is the Principal or other popular teacher). **(4)** The Principal has specifically requested the District/Division Crisis Team or members to provide support to the School-based Crisis Team. The request may be made directly when it is imperative that crisis members come to the school immediately, or the Principal may complete the **Critical Incident Intervention Request** located in **Appendix 3** and submit it to the appropriate official. In many areas District/Division Crisis Teams are not dispatched to schools unless specifically requested by the Principal of the affected school. The community sees the Principal in charge of the school and ultimately responsible for the actions taken and avoided. This empowers the School-based Crisis Team and instills confidence in their ability. Specific checklists have been included (**Appendices 2 and 3**), to help track actions taken by School Based Crisis Team personnel when a critical incident occurs. According to information from the Delta School District (1997), responses at the school and department may include the following:

- ### *School-Based Response to Crises*
  - ▸ Will actively implement the school based crisis response plan.
  - ▸ Will actively request assistance from the District/Division Crisis Response Team, if needed. This determination should be made by the Principal in consultation with other members of the school-based crisis response team.
  - ▸ Will conduct such activities as defusing emotions, classroom debriefings, and crisis counseling.
  - ▸ Will prepare an information letter to parents.
  - ▸ Will conduct crisis response team and staff debriefings.
  - ▸ Will provide a statement to the media providing information about actions taken at the school.
  - ▸ Will monitor and coordinate all crisis response activities at the school.

- ## *District/Division Response to Crises*
  - ▷ Will actively provide additional assistance to the school-based crisis response team, if requested by the Principal of the affected school.
  - ▷ Will actively request assistance from government departments and sources, if necessary.
  - ▷ Will contact the school bus company informing them of the incident and any scheduling changes as well as alerting them to possible differences in student behavior while on the buses.
  - ▷ Will contact all feeder schools with information about the incident.
  - ▷ Will provide information to the media about actions taken by the District/Division Crisis Response Team to the incident.
  - ▷ Will maintain close contact with the affected school.
  - ▷ Will dispatch the District/Division Crisis Team or members to schools that do not have school-based crisis teams or if the school crisis team is in a crisis state.
  - ▷ Will conduct District/Division level debriefing for central office staff to evaluate the response at that level.

- ## *Emergency Support*

This is the level of intervention whereby external crisis response members, e.g. District/Division crisis response members, take a secondary role to the school-based crisis teams members when intervening in a critical incident. The school-based crisis team members are responsible for the implementation of individual and classroom debriefings. District/Division crisis team members provide psychological support to the school-based team members and are available should school-based members get into difficulty dealing with individual questions and/or situations. External responders should take a secondary role to any school-based crisis team member unless directed otherwise by the Principal.

WHAT SCHOOLS MUST ADDRESS

Petersen & Straub (1992), state that schools are incredibly influential in the daily lives of families within the community. Often a great deal of the discipline and nurturing needed to raise a son or daughter centers around their life at school. Even parents who do not take an active interest in the school on a daily or regular basis have a silent interest in the school's environment as it affects their sons and daughters. Thus the school becomes an effective and integral force within the community and in every family. For some children it is the only source of safety and stability. Today, schools are expected to address more than academic and intellectual needs of students; increasing emphasis is being placed upon the emotional, social, and physical needs of the students. Parents are beginning to look more to schools for the back-up support previously offered by the extended family. It is important to understand that it takes time to resolve a traumatic event. Calling in departmental and community specialists to help deal with the crisis is a good practice; however, work with affected students must continue after the external consultants have returned to their offices. It is then up to the school to provide a constant and consistent support system for students. After a few days most students will not need help, but some will require ongoing counseling and support to prevent Post Traumatic Stress Disorder. It is important to note that the ongoing counseling differs from what is usually offered at the guidance office and what is available during the crisis. Quick intervention is a far more effective means to recovery than spending hours in a psychologist's office after the fact.

The importance of students' identification with the school is reflected in less school vandalism, lower dropout rate, and higher academic achievement. When crises and other traumatic events are not adequately resolved they interfere with a student's acceptance of the school identity. Likewise, precedents have already been set in court where school boards have been held liable for not adequately protecting the student and have been ordered to pay compensation. In an effort to protect the school, every crisis must be evaluated for possible liability. However, through implementation of a school-based crisis intervention plan, the administration at the school will demonstrate that it is prepared to protect children during crises and other traumatic events.

LIABILITY

Schools are not subject to specific laws that require them to provide specialized services in the aftermath of a crisis; however, implementing classroom debriefings attends to issues of legal, moral, and ethical importance. These issues directly concern the role of the school and behavior of school personnel. It is wise that school-based crisis response team members follow departmental/divisional policy and procedures, direction from the school division's solicitor, and their own professional judgment when attempting to meet students' needs during a crisis. Crisis teams and/or individual team members who engage in "freelancing" during a crisis may be harmful to the overall mission of the crisis team. In an effort to protect the school, every crisis must be evaluated for possible liability. If there is any doubt, check with the departmental/divisional solicitor. Crisis team members are well advised to remember that today we live in a litigious society. Often lawsuits are considered remedy. A lawsuit can be filed against anyone at almost anytime and for just about any reason if a plaintiff feels that a personal wrong or injury has been caused. These lawsuits are brought under civil law.

Unless a crisis team member has a preexisting duty to provide assistance or intervene in another person's crisis, the law usually does not require that anyone intervene in the crisis of anyone else. However, once an individual has started an intervention, that person must continue with the intervention unless relieved by someone with greater skill and ability. If the crisis team member does not continue with the intervention it may constitute abandonment, which could bring legal consequences. Negligence may occur when a crisis team member intervenes in the crisis of an individual but breaches that intervention, thus causing damage or further injury to the victim. In some areas "Good Samaritan" laws may protect individuals who intervene on behalf of those in a state of crisis; the intervention, however, must be reasonable and prudent. If it is not, negligence may occur.

Another area of concern to school-based and district/divisional crisis response team members is the issue of confidentiality. It is important to note that various statutes regulate the collection, use, and disclosure of information by School Boards and Departments. The facts of each case of critical incident will determine when it is legally appropriate to collect, use, and disclose personal information and to whom that information may be disclosed.

Specific Acts that regulate the disclosure of information include the **ACCESS TO INFORMATION AND PROTECTION OF PRIVACY ACT**, which applies to all provinces and territories in Canada. This Act restricts the collection and disclosure of written personal information by Boards and regulates the storage of such information. Note that personal information related to a deceased person is still covered by this Act. The second type of act to be considered is the **YOUNG OFFENDERS ACT**. Written copies of announcements, notices, letter of information to parents, and press releases about critical incidents need to be written carefully to meet the requirements of legislation relevant to the young offender. *This Act limits the publication of the names of the young offender. It is particularly noteworthy if a critical incident results from an offence.* This Act states that *no report can be published respecting the offence committed or alleged to have been committed by a young person*, in which the name of the young alleged perpetrator or the name of the young victim or witness is mentioned. Disclosures to any professional or person engaged in supervisory care of a young person, a representative of any school board or school, or any other educational or training institution can only be made if it is necessary to ensure the safety of staff, students, and other persons. Keeping a written record of this type of information is also subject to the aforementioned requirements. All information should be handled and stored so that individual confidentiality is not compromised.

The last area includes the use of **E-MAIL** messages sent via government computers. These are considered property of the Government and are subject to the **ACCESS TO INFORMATION AND PROTECTION OF PRIVACY ACT**. When using e-mail between schools or departments *it is wise to remember that all e-mail messages are on record.* Keep your communication confidential by not mentioning client names.

WHAT IS A CRISIS?

• *Crisis Reaction*

According to Fairchild (1986), "a crisis is a period of psychological imbalance, which is experienced in the face of a hazardous or traumatizing event, which can neither be escaped nor solved with customary problem-solving behaviors." It is important to remember that any change creates stress. Depending on an individual's past experience and coping skills, they will either successfully meet the challenges of change or become overwhelmed by the challenges and will be in an active crisis state. It can thus be said that a crisis is not necessarily an event, but an individual's perception of an event as being both dangerous and threatening. It is something the individual cannot succeed, or has not succeeded in resolving, removing, avoiding, or controlling.

• *Crisis Intervention*

Fairchild (1986) defines crisis intervention as the process whereby helpers attempt to restore psychological equilibrium by improving the individual's coping skills and offering new alternatives for handling the troubling situation.

• *Origins Of Crises*

Crises, as defined by Fairchild (1986), are an inevitable part of human existence occurring often in the lives of individuals and their families. He goes on to state that the origin of crises fall into three major categories.

1. **Situational or Unanticipated**

> Material/environmental (fire or natural disaster);

> Personal/physical (heart attack, fatal illness, loss of a limb);

> Interpersonal/social (death of a loved one, divorce);

2. **Transitional or Anticipated**

> Universal (life cycle, normal transitions in human development);

> Non-universal (changing jobs, retirement, moving);

3.　Social Origins

> ⊳　Violation of social norms (sexual assault, abuse, robbery, assault).

- ### *Avoiding A Crisis*

A crisis does not occur instantly; a process or series of developments must be present for a crisis or a crisis state to exist. At times all that may be required is emotional support. Weeping openly and expressing sorrow are not signs that the individual is in an active crisis state. It is possible to exacerbate an existing situation and turn it into a critical incident by over-responding to the situation.

Note
A potentially hazardous or traumatizing event is <u>not</u> by itself evidence that a crisis or crisis state exists, Fairchild (1986). Individuals responding to a critical incident must always guard against the possibility of <u>creating</u> a crisis when in fact one does <u>not</u> exist.

According to Fairchild (1986), if the following condition occurs a crisis may be avoided:

> ⊳　There must be a hazardous event, which intrudes on the lives of individuals.
> ⊳　Individuals or groups must perceive the event as important and threatening, thereby causing a state of tension and anxiety.
> ⊳　Emotional reactions to the event occur.
> ⊳　Individuals experiencing the tension rely on their customary coping behaviors in an attempt to resolve the situation.
> ⊳　These behaviors relieve the tension, thus an internal state of psychological equilibrium is maintained.
> ⊳　The hazardous event is resolved and emotional discomfort is alleviated.
> ⊳　Individuals have successfully dealt with the event through the use of familiar coping skills.
> ⊳　Individuals remain unchanged with no prolonged behavioral or emotional disturbance.

A crisis is avoided.

DEVELOPMENT OF A CRISIS STATE

Fairchild (1986), states that a crisis is an event that always combines both the potential for danger and an opportunity for growth. **Dange**r exists when the event creates a level of emotional discomfort that cannot be relieved through the use of customary coping behaviors and skills. **Growth** exists when individuals seek help from friends or other persons and as a result acquire new or more effective coping skills when dealing with a critical incident.

If the following sequence of events occurs, Fairchild (1986) indicates that a crisis state exists:

- The hazardous event creates a level of emotional discomfort that cannot be relieved through the use of customary coping skills.
- The event is seen as important and threatening to individuals.
- Emotional reaction occurs in response to the incident.
- Normal coping behaviors are employed to deal with the incident.
- Normal coping behaviors are not effective.
- Individuals continue to employ ineffective coping behaviors to deal with the incident.
- Disorganization and psychological imbalance occur. .
- Internal discomfort increases in intensity, both cognitive and emotional distortion occurs. **Cognitive distortion** refers to the inability to deal with reality, plan, and predict consequences. **Emotional distortion** refers to individual emotional reactivity, heightened feelings of helplessness, and the feeling that the situation is hopeless.
- Turmoil intensifies.
- The emotional discomfort is so debilitating that it takes the form of physical symptoms such as insomnia, regressive behaviors, and withdrawal.
- A state of disorganization and psychological imbalance follows which reduces problem-solving capacity.

> Individuals are now in a state of active crisis because their present problem remains unresolved and the range of emotions that they are experiencing has risen to an unbearable degree.

> Individuals take action to relieve the turmoil.

> The situation cannot be resolved; individuals are in an active crisis state.

• _Duration Of Crises_

Crises are limited in duration, lasting from two or three days to a few months. Most critical incidents tend to last approximately two days to a week. By the third day there are signs of routine and structure in the daily activities. In any event there should be a follow-up scheduled approximately two weeks after the initial incident. Consequences are long-term. They may be either **adaptive** (improved coping skills) or **maladaptive** (continued use of maladaptive coping skills). In the latter case the individual has not learned any new skills to use the next time he/she is exposed to a traumatic event.

• _Outcomes Of Crises_

Individuals exposed to a crisis will return to one of four possible outcomes. The outcome is dependent, in part, on whether the school has implemented an effective crisis plan, whether the effected students have participated in individual or group debriefings, defusing or group discussions, and whether they have accessed support at home.

1. Individuals return to the pre-crisis state, but may experience Post Traumatic Stress Disorder.

2. Individuals return to the pre-crisis state but grow from the experience through acquiring new coping and problem-solving behaviors and skills.

3. Individuals return to the pre-crisis state but do not grow from the experience or acquire new coping and problem-solving behaviors and skills.

4. Individuals lapse into neurotic or psychotic patterns of behavior.

SUCCESSFUL CRISIS MANAGEMENT

If a traumatic event does develop, the immediate reaction and future consequences of the event on students and staff depend upon how quickly and effectively the school crisis team and staff respond to the situation. Immediate action is essential if staff is to maintain leadership and control throughout the incident. Successful management of a crisis tends to follow five specific steps.

1. **Assessment Of The Crisis**

   School-based helpers need to first determine whether individuals are, in fact, in a state of crisis. The School-Based Crisis Team should determine the level of need and support. Care must be taken when looking for links to other individuals or situations. There is always the potential to develop a crisis state when in fact none exits.

2. **Development Of An Intervention Plan**

   Only after helpers have a thorough understanding of the nature of the incident and its severity, can they begin to formulate a plan of action. Crisis intervention should be short-term in nature. Maintenance strategies are most important. These are strategies that prevent the situation from deteriorating and the individuals' mental/physical health from declining further.

3. **Implementation Of The Intervention Plan**

   This will require direction by school-based crisis team members. It is important to set achievable goals that can be obtained in small steps.

4. **Ongoing Evaluation And Modification Of The Plan**

   Helpers should keep a record of the assessment information gathered. This should include working notes, a list of goals that have been identified for resolving the crisis, a list of various activities, strategies that helpers have implemented, and a record of the effectiveness of the various strategies used.

5. <u>Post-Crisis Follow-Up</u>

It is important to follow-up with individual assessment after the crisis has passed. This assures helpers that effected individuals have satisfactorily resolved their crisis. This also assures individuals who experienced difficulty coping that people care about them.

RECORD KEEPING

With some students the intervention plans may be verbal; however, it is a good idea to keep accurate, written records when working with students in crisis. This is especially important today because schools are held increasingly liable for providing support services to children who are experiencing a crisis. Documentation provides some evidence that specific and appropriate intervention has taken place. It is easy to forget what has been said or suggested to a student or group, particularly during a crisis. Recording the date and nature of the incident is important for monitoring the anniversary date and individual responses at that time. Written records will also be helpful should there be legal concerns or questions about strategies and interventions implemented at the school. As well, written records and checklists provide an excellent source of information for reviewing and revising the school crisis plan.

- ***Completing the Forms***

Information that should be recorded includes:

1. Record of the assessment information gathered during the first interview.
2. The names of the students contacted during the crisis.
3. List of goals and solutions students identified for resolving the crisis.
4. Lists of all activities and strategies students and teachers will implement.
5. To make the task of tracking information easier. Record the effectiveness of all the strategies used. A number of forms have been specifically developed and are located in **Appendices 2** and **3**.

6. Detailed information about the event and date that it occurred, date of the memorial service, identity of those most affected, as well as closest friends and relatives of the victim.

7. It is most important to record the exact date of the incident or death so as to be prepared for changes in behavior on the anniversary of the incident.

8. Keep all completed forms and checklists for future reference. This information is evidence that action was taken at the school.

Note: It is the responsibility of the Principal in collaboration with the school-based crisis team to determine which forms, checklists, and logs may be used, modified, or deleted during a critical incident. Completion of the form provides a record of specific strategies, procedures, and actions taken during a critical incident. They also provide documented evidence that may be beneficial to the school-based crisis team in the face of potential litigation.

PART 3. SCHOOL-BASED CRISIS TEAM IN ACTION

SEQUENCE OF EVENTS

When a traumatic incident occurs there usually is a predictable sequence of events that follows the incident. The most traumatic time is ***during the first day*** with normalcy beginning to return around the third day. During these three days anyone affected by the incident will be on an emotional roller coaster. A short description of these first three days is presented below.

Day 1

This will be the most emotional day for staff and students. The needs of staff should be met first so they can effectively meet student needs. During the first day defusing emotions, group discussions, classroom debriefings, student and staff counseling, setting up a student drop-in center, assigning hall monitors, and the preparation of an information letter to be sent to all parents are some of the more important activities. Staff meetings should occur before and after school so that school staff is kept completely informed about crisis, the response taken by the school crisis team and the resources available to everyone. It is important to include all secretarial and custodial staff in these meetings. Students most at risk should be identified. Reduced structure and routine should be expected in most classrooms, especially the victim's classroom(s). Teachers should attempt to maintain some degree of structure and routine in order to help keep students focused on the activities and not on the crisis.

Day 2

The second day may not be as emotionally intense as the first. Student and staff counseling activities should continue. Students may continue to attend discussion groups and defusing sessions. Classroom activities may focus on helping students cope with and grieve the loss. The classroom teacher should start to deal with the personal effects of the deceased student, in the event of a student death. Additional students at risk should be identified. A staff debriefing should be conducted on this day or the next. Teachers should continue to maintain a degree of structure and routine in their classrooms.

Day 3

Some signs of closure should start to appear; however, there may be an increase in emotionality due to the pending memorial and the fact that some students may participate in a service for the deceased. [If a death is due to suicide, a memorial is not recommended. If there is strong opposition by students to the school not participating in some form of memorial for the deceased, the service should be small. It is important not to glorify a suicide in any way.] Student and staff counseling should continue. Students most at risk should continue to be assisted. There should be increased structure and routine in all classrooms. Follow-up activities should be scheduled for approximately two weeks after the traumatic incident, with a second follow-up about six weeks after that. A crisis team debriefing should be conducted within the next week or two.

INITIAL ASSESSMENT

The onset of a crisis is a stressful time for all school staff. When the school-based crisis team is called into action at the school to deal with a critical incident, it enables teaching staff to concentrate on maintaining routine and stability for students. In order for a school-based crisis team to intervene effectively, helpers must first determine whether students are, in fact, in a crisis state.

The initial assessment should occur immediately and not over a period of days. This assessment should focus on immediate and identifiable concerns of students and must evaluate the risk to life, because there is potential danger to life when an individual is in an active state of crisis. Helpers must remember that the assessment is not something that is done to the individual, but is a counseling/interviewing process carried out with individuals through their active participation. This process may also include collaboration with significant others. Only after members of the school crisis team have conducted the initial assessment and have an understanding of the nature of the incident and its severity, can they begin to develop an effective plan. Caution is advised when conducting the assessment because there is always the potential to develop a crisis state when in fact none exits.

Note - *It **cannot** be presumed that individuals who are extremely emotionally upset are in a state of crisis. School-based helpers need to remember that the critical ingredient for a crisis state to exist is that in addition to being emotionally upset, individuals have **exhausted** their coping resources. They are at the point where they are experiencing severe emotional turmoil and can **no longer** cope effectively using their adaptive coping behaviors (Fairchild, 1986).*

- ## *Immediate Team Responsibilities*

The school based crisis team has numerous functions that are divided into three time frames: **pre-crisis**, **crisis**, and **post-crisis**. When developing and adapting the crisis plan there are certain components and procedures that should be considered for each time frame. If they are followed, the crisis plan will operate much more effectively. As well, by following the plan in a systematic manner, you are less likely to forget a contact that should have been dealt with during the initial stages of the incident (Petersen & Straub, 1992). Immediate responsibilities for the school based crisis team are presented below.

1. Assemble the team and verify information;
2. Contact area superintendent;
3. Adapt the plan to fit the current crisis;
4. Meet with school staff and announce event;
5. Request additional support from District/Divisional Crisis Team, if deemed necessary;
6. Assign staff roles and responsibilities;
   - Principal.
   - Counselors.
   - Teachers.
   - School Psychologist.
   - Secretary/school support staff.
7. Set up student drop-in center (secondary schools)
8. Set up a Crisis Center.
9. Designate a person to whom all information will be sent and recorded.
10. Assign hallway and washroom monitors;
11. Assist or provide crisis counseling and debriefing;

12. Write an information release for the media and an information letter to parents;

13. Hire extra help for the front office;

14. Hire substitute teachers familiar with the school;

15. Notify the school bus company of the event;

16. Gather information regarding the memorial;

17. Schedule staff debriefing at later date, usually within the first three days.

- ### *Checking The Facts*

Many school systems have developed a liaison with their local police departments or coroner to ensure that they are contacted when an incident affecting the school occurs. This can be most helpful because it allows the school to put its crisis plan into effect promptly. In the face of serious trauma, rumours can run rampant. Establishing a line of communication with the police **before** an emergency arises assures that the facts are received and rumours are dispelled, thus alleviating anxiety and uncertainty. Initially establishing this line of communication may be difficult. Police departments are concerned with notifying the next of kin, as well as guarding against the premature release of any information that may be presented in court (Petersen & Straub, 1992). Once the initial tasks of checking the facts and assembling the crisis team have been completed, the team should concentrate on developing or adapting the crisis plan to the current situation. Before doing so verify the basic facts.

1. Who was/were the victim(s)?

2. How did he/she/they die? Accident? Suicide? Illness?

3. When did he/she/they die? Where?

4. Did anyone witness the death(s)? Who?

5. Who were close friends of the victim(s)?

6. How was/were the death(s) discovered? By Whom?

7. Do(es) the victim(s) have siblings or relatives attending different schools?

- ### *Adapting The Plan To Fit The Crisis*

There is more than one way to respond to a crisis when it develops. The crisis team should have a sound understanding of the various crisis intervention techniques. They may be required to alter or modify their procedures and strategies, depending on the nature and scope of the situation. The goal of any crisis intervention is to prevent further trauma to children and prevent Post Traumatic Stress Disorder. When adapting the intervention plan consider these points.

How Will The Announcement Be Made?

> Can you tell your school staff first?

> Is this a school wide crisis?

> Do you need to request additional support from the District/Division?

> Can you announce the event in such a way that it does not become sensationalized?

> Will rumors and speculation result because of the way the announcement is made?

> How do you expect the staff, students, and the parents to react to the news?

> Who should be notified within your school system?

Will A Memorial Service Be Held?

> How wide spread is the effect of this tragedy on your students?

> Is this an incident that should be memorialized at the school?

> Will the service be open to the public, the press, or parents?

> Set the date, time, and location of any school memorial service.

> Are the parents of the deceased supportive of a school memorial service?

> Are there any special religious considerations that must be observed?

Does The School Have Any Legal Responsibility?

> How will you inform parents?

> Has an information letter for parents been prepared?

> What supports, if any will you provide for parents?

> Are students or staff likely to face bouts of depression? How will you prepare them?

> Who can you contact from your school board or community for assistance?

How Will You Address The Media?

- ▷ Who is your spokesperson? This should be the Principal, or another person as pre-determined through Divisional/District policy.
- ▷ Is this incident likely to draw national attention?
- ▷ Has a written statement for the press been prepared?
- ▷ Has a time and a location been set to meet with the media? Where will this take place?

How Much Staff Support Is Needed?

- ▷ Is it necessary to provide counseling for staff?
- ▷ Who will provide this faculty support?
- ▷ Have a time and location been established to meet with the staff after the school day?
- ▷ Is **Employee Assistance Program** counseling available to staff?

CONTACTING SCHOOL STAFF

Staff notification depends a great deal upon when the news of the event breaks. If possible, sensitive information should be delivered in person. Establishing a **Telephone Contact Tree** whereby each staff member has three names to call provides a pre-established avenue of communication (Petersen & Straub, 1992). When time allows, this method can be used to arrange a staff meeting before school. The staff can then be personally informed of the tragedy when they are together at the meeting (for example, before classes begin in the morning). This approach provides the greatest support and it most effectively reduces rumors. However, if time does not allow a staff meeting before school, then, the news of the event can be given directly to the staff through the telephone tree. If the crisis occurs during the instructional day, the principal may consider calling the crisis team to the office and then sending members back to systematically inform their colleagues. The principal might speak to the teachers individually and/or send a **Critical Incident Alert Form** to each teacher informing him/her of the basic facts of the incident. Informing the staff first helps to maintain maximum control over the reaction of staff and students because the information given is accurate and consistent. Teachers should also have an opportunity to release some of their own grief and offer comfort to each other before they begin to support others.

It is important to schedule another meeting with the staff at the end of the day after the students have left, to discuss the events and reactions which occurred during the day and to inform them of what might be expected the following day. Giving support to so many children for an entire day is very draining. Teachers also create emotional bonds with their students and are thereby affected by the loss. Allow time to discuss ways they might recover from the crisis before facing the students again the next day. Have the counselor or school psychologist brief teachers on what to expect of the students during the next few weeks and explain how the teachers can help. The support you provide for your staff at this time will enhance cohesion amongst the student body as well.

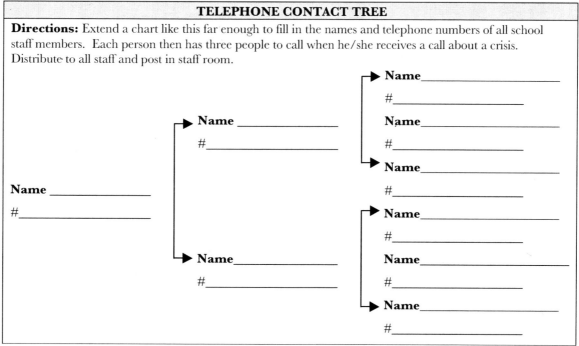

TELEPHONE CONTACT TREE

Directions: Extend a chart like this far enough to fill in the names and telephone numbers of all school staff members. Each person then has three people to call when he/she receives a call about a crisis. Distribute to all staff and post in staff room.

Adapted from Petersen, S. & Straub, R.L. (1992)

MAKING THE ANNOUNCEMENT IN SCHOOL

The announcement to staff and students must convey the facts of the incident in a sensitive and compassionate manner. Keep in mind the fight-or-flight response to trauma. The announcement should be made in a way that will contain this intense emotional reaction. In the event that there are individuals known to be especially close to the victim, the news should be delivered in private. The public address system should **not** be used to announce the death of a student. Teachers should make this announcement in their classrooms. Only when a loss is considered to be school-wide should use of the public address system be considered. Sample announcements are provided below, Petersen & Straub (1992).

- ### *Sample Announcements*

In classroom (individual child's loss)

_____ will not be in school today. His/her father was killed in a vehicle accident last night. A truck struck his car on the Alaska Highway. _____ will be very sad for a long time. Perhaps we can discuss some ways _____ might be feeling and how we can all help him/her.

In classroom (school-wide loss)

We have something very sad to tell you today. _____ was driving home in the rain last night. His/her car swerved into an oncoming lane, was struck by another car and went off the road. _____ died in the crash. It was sudden and he/she did not suffer.

Over public address system (school-wide loss)

Our school has suffered a great, great loss. _____, the science teacher, has been ill with cancer for many months now. We just received word that his/her suffering has come to an end and _____ has died. We will be commemorating _____'s contribution to our school community. At this time, I'd like each class to discuss the ways they would like to commemorate the life work of _____.

In classroom (declared suicide)

We are sad to announce that _____ took his life last night. His family will make memorial service arrangements. Counseling will be provided for those who wish to speak with a counselor. It is always a shock when we hear of someone taking his/her life. Let's cancel work this morning to discuss this.

In classroom (undeclared suicide or fact has not been made public)

_____ died last night of a gunshot wound. He/she apparently had a gun in his/her hand when it fired. Counseling will be provided for those who wish to speak with someone. When an unexpected incident such as this occurs, it helps to discuss it. Regular class work will be canceled to allow time for discussion.

STAFF ROLES AND RESPONSIBILITIES

The school-based Crisis team leader (this should be the Principal), should inform the entire staff about their responsibilities during a crisis. This action alone reduces much of the staff anxiety and instills in them the confidence needed to support the students. Discussing staff responsibilities prior to a crisis allows time for expression of dissension and helps to guarantee that the follow-through the team has decided upon will take place during an actual crisis. Suggested roles and responsibilities as adapted from Petersen & Straub (1992) follow:

- ***Principal***
    - ▹ Contact area Superintendent.
    - ▹ Verify the accuracy of the information from the police.
    - ▹ Activate the School-Based Crisis Team.
    - ▹ Meet with staff to announce the event before school starts.
    - ▹ Determine if support is needed from the District/Division.
    - ▹ Determine if additional resources are needed.
    - ▹ Remain highly visible.
    - ▹ Set tone and direction.
    - ▹ Chair crisis team.
    - ▹ Meet with staff after school.
    - ▹ Contact other schools if necessary.
    - ▹ Set time and location to meet with the media. Prepare a statement for the media.
    - ▹ Prepare information letter to be sent to all parents.
    - ▹ State clear procedures for secretarial staff responding to calls or requests from parents, media, or others.
    - ▹ If appropriate, call the clergy to be available for counseling.
    - ▹ Cancel scheduled activities.
    - ▹ Seek additional secretarial support.

- ## *Counselor*
  - ▷ Provide counseling services for students.
  - ▷ Plan logistics of counseling.
  - ▷ Lead debriefings, defusing sessions, and group discussions.
  - ▷ Establish the student drop-in center.
  - ▷ Coordinate all counseling activities in the school.
  - ▷ Communicate with teaching staff and principal.
  - ▷ Seek additional counseling support.
  - ▷ Provide information to parents.
  - ▷ Identify students most at risk.

- ## *Teachers*
  - ▷ Announce event to the students in their classrooms.
  - ▷ Lead class discussions/debriefings.
  - ▷ Identify students in need of counseling.
  - ▷ Allow students to go to Drop-In Center.
  - ▷ Identify students most likely needing support (e.g., close relatives, friends of victim).
  - ▷ Generate activities to reduce the impact of trauma.
  - ▷ Structure and shorten assignments.
  - ▷ Postpone testing.
  - ▷ Request additional support if needed.
  - ▷ Deal with victim's personal belongings.
  - ▷ Network with colleagues for support.
  - ▷ Monitor own needs.
  - ▷ Maintain structure and routine in the classroom.

- ***Secretary***
  - ▷ Maintain telephone log of all calls from parents, media, and other schools about the event.
  - ▷ Give only approved information as determined by the Crisis Response Team; refer to official spokesperson if one is appointed.
  - ▷ Type prepared information letters to parents.
  - ▷ Escort parents who arrive at the school to the reception area.
  - ▷ Ensure parents and staff have access to coffee, tea, and food.
  - ▷ Attend all meetings; record minutes as advised by Principal.
  - ▷ Contact external agencies as advised.
  - ▷ Meet all media personnel at front door and escort to and from scheduled meetings.
  - ▷ Maintain student sign in/out log.
  - ▷ Contact parents as directed by the Principal.
  - ▷ Maintain record of all individuals coming in to the school.
  - ▷ Identify and refer students at risk.
  - ▷ Take time for yourself.

- ***School Psychologists***
  - ▷ Provide support and counseling to staff.
  - ▷ Conduct student counseling as directed.
  - ▷ Lead debriefings, defusing sessions, and group discussions when requested.
  - ▷ Monitor students in hallways and other unsupervised areas.
  - ▷ Assist principal with letter to parents if requested.
  - ▷ Provide information (Post Traumatic Stress Disorder/Debriefings) to students and staff.
  - ▷ Meet with concerned parents if requested.

- ***Support Staff***
  - ▷ Follow crisis intervention plan.
  - ▷ Attend all staff meetings.

> Request support when needed.

> Identify and refer students at risk.

> Maintain professionalism.

> Respect confidentiality.

> Know who is in the building

CLASSROOM ACTIVITIES

Teachers did not choose education as a career to deal with crisis issues. They will need some reassurance that they are capable of handling the students, the critical incident, and that they are doing a good job. Suggestions for age-appropriate classroom activities follow in the next section and can be reviewed when the staff discusses their responsibilities.

PRESCHOOL ACTIVITIES

Creative classroom activities may be helpful to teachers seeking ways to deal with the stress and tension of a crisis and its effects on students. The following activities are vehicles for expression and discussion for students, and are important steps in helping them handle the stress they are experiencing. You can use these activities to stimulate your own ideas and adapt them to meet both your students' needs and your teaching style (Johnson, 1993).

1. Make available toys that encourage play enactment of the child's concerns. Such toys might include airplanes, helicopters, toy police officers, rescue trucks, ambulances, building blocks, puppets, or dolls. Playing with these toys allows the child to ventilate feelings about what is occurring or has already occurred.

2. Children need lots of physical contact during times of stress to help them re-establish their sense of security. Introduce *structured* games that involve physical touching among children.

3. Provide extra amounts of drinks and finger foods in small portions. This is a concrete way of supplying the emotional and physical nourishment children need in times of

stress. Oral satisfaction is especially necessary because children tend to exhibit more regressive behaviors in response to feelings that threaten their survival or security.

4. Have the children make a mural, using topics related to what is happening in the world and in their community. This is recommended for small groups, with discussion afterwards facilitated by the teacher or other skilled adult.

5. Have the children draw individual pictures about the crisis situation and then discuss the pictures in small groups. This activity allows children to vent their experiences and to discover that others share their fears.

6. Make a group collage, and discuss what the collage represents, how it was made, and the feelings it evokes.

- ***Helper's Response to Preschool/Kindergarten Students***

GOAL
⊳ Reestablish trust and security.
⊳ Reestablish self-control and autonomy.

METHOD
⊳ Provide physical comforts (e.g. warm milk, cuddling or holding the child, food).
⊳ Reestablish structure and routines.
⊳ Assure and provide adult protection.
⊳ Let parents know that it is 'OK' for the child to temporarily sleep in their room.
⊳ Help child draw, act out, and discuss incident.
⊳ Clarify event, misconceptions, and misunderstandings.
⊳ Be calm.

ELEMENTARY SCHOOL ACTIVITIES

1. For younger children, make toys available that encourage play to express concerns, fears, and observations. These toys might include ambulances, planes, tanks, helicopters, toy police officers, rescue vehicles, toy soldiers, building blocks, and dolls. Play with puppets can provide ways for older children, as well as younger children, to ventilate their feelings (Johnson, 1993).

2. Help or encourage children to develop skits or puppet shows about what happened during the crisis. Encourage them to include anything positive about the experience as well as frightening or disconcerting aspects.

3. Have the children create short stories about the crisis and how it was managed. These stories can be either written or dictated to an adult, depending on the age of the child.

4. Have the children draw pictures and discuss them in relation to the crisis. It is important that the group discussion end on a positive note.

5. Stimulate group discussion about the crisis and its consequences by showing your own feelings or fears. It is very important to legitimize children's feelings and to help them feel less isolated. It is equally important to give them a sense of structure, balance, and control over their own activities and life.

6. Have the children brainstorm their own ways of handling their concerns. Encourage them to discuss the results with their parents.

7. Encourage class activities in which the children can organize and build projects, such as scrapbooks, to give them a sense of mastery and ability to organize what seems to be chaotic and confusing.

8. Encourage children to talk about their feelings about the crisis.

• ***Helper's Response to Elementary Students***

GOAL

> Bolster self-esteem.

> Relieve guilt.

> Reestablish productivity.

> Provide reassurances of safety.

METHOD

> Encourage expression of thoughts and feelings.

> Validate normalcy of reaction.

> Reestablish structure and routines.

> Lessen requirements for optimal performance.

> Reinforce age-appropriate behavior.

> ꝺ   Provide structure as behavior indicates.

> ꝺ   Allow expression of feelings of responsibility; clarify misconceptions.

JUNIOR/SENIOR HIGH SCHOOL ACTIVITIES

The following suggestions could be carried out within specific courses at the school. Teachers are encouraged to expand these suggestions to fit the students' needs and the teachers' individual styles (Johnson, 1993).

1. Conduct a group discussion of the students' experiences concerning the crisis situation and the events surrounding it. This is particularly important to adolescents because they need the opportunity to vent as well as to normalize the extreme emotions that arise. A good way to stimulate such a discussion is to share your personal reactions. The students may need considerable reassurance that even extreme emotions and 'crazy' thoughts are normal under these circumstances. It is important to end the discussions on a positive note. Such discussions are appropriate for any course of study because it can hasten the return to more normal functioning.

2. Conduct a class discussion or support a class project on how students might involve themselves in activities related to managing the crisis. This might include support groups, rallies, and assistance to family members. It is important to help students develop concrete, realistic ways to assist or be involved. This helps them to overcome the feelings of helplessness, frustration, and guilt, common reactions to these situations.

3. Introduce classroom activities that relate the crisis and its consequences to the course of study. This can be an effective way to help students integrate their own experiences or observations while providing specific learning experiences. When performing these activities, it is important to allow time for students to discuss the feelings stimulated by the projects or the other issues covered.

- ### *Helper's Response to Junior/Senior High Students*

GOAL

- ‣ Inoculate against secondary reactions.
- ‣ Emphasize stress management.
- ‣ Facilitate identity development.
- ‣ Reaffirm life direction.

METHOD

- ‣ Encourage discussion and expression.
- ‣ Validate normalcy of reaction.
- ‣ Reestablish structure and routines.
- ‣ Lessen requirements for optimal performance.
- ‣ Provide opportunity for positive action.
- ‣ Provide monitoring, guidance.
- ‣ Provide conceptualization of incident, reactions, and situation.

TEACHER DO'S AND DON'TS

During a critical incident many teachers are concerned about what they should say and do in the classroom. Not knowing what to say or do is often the cause of considerable stress and anxiety for the teacher. Clayton (1994), in her *Crisis Intervention Guide*, provides a number of suggestions, which are listed below.

DO'S

1. Feel comfortable in asking for help because you do not have to handle the experience alone.
2. Use the correct, concrete terminology. Avoid using such euphemisms as "gone to asleep, long journey" etc.
3. Use age appropriate language.
4. Tell the truth about the incident without unnecessary details.
5. Development an environment in which students feel safe to discuss and question.
6. Give honest answers.

7. Listen and empathize.

8. Remember to share your own feelings.

9. Allow your students to express as much grief as they are willing to share with you.

10. Allow students to release strong feelings of anger and bitterness about what they are feeling.

11. Remember to say, "I don't know" if that is the case.

12. Organize activities that will allow students to tangibly express their grief.

13. Be flexible about your normal classroom routine.

14. Note any student who is having significant difficulty coping and report to the counselor and parents.

15. Share with the class the opportunity to collect the deceased's belongings.

16. Don't forget to carefully edit all messages, letters, and cards sent by students to a grieving family for appropriateness.

DON'TS

1. Don't immediately remove all evidence of a deceased student's or teacher's presence in the classroom.

2. Do not deal in rumors or speculation. If asked personal, sensitive, or embarrassing questions about the death, stick to the facts only. Do not get into descriptive or gory details about the death.

3. Don's use philosophical, religious, or sentimental references.

4. Don't make individual participation in classroom discussions mandatory.

5. Don't lecture, moralize, or cast judgment.

6. Don't link suffering and death with guilt, punishment, and sin.

7. Don't expect adult responses from students, even teenagers.

8. Don't ridicule or belittle any questions.

9. Don't force others to look for something positive in the tragedy.

10. Don't say, "I know how you feel."

11. Don't force a regular day on grieving students.

PART 4. DEALING WITH THE MEDIA AND PARENTS

This section assumes that the principal will be the one responsible for dealing with the media. In some districts/divisions, there are assigned communication staff who control release of information and provide general information to the press about the event and actions taken by the District/Division. In any case, the following information should be helpful for who-ever is responsible for dealing with the media. Principals will be responsible for dealing with parents, but may choose to seek support from district/divisional communication staff.

The wise Principal will **"be prepared for public scrutiny."** Once you have developed a good working relationship with the press, you are in a much stronger position. The media can then become an extension of your communication from the school. This can work to the school's advantage in that the press can help spread the word to the community as a whole.

According to Johnson (1993), principals consistently report that the media is the most difficult part of handling a crisis. The responsibility to protect students and to respond to community's concerns is enormous. This area, more than any other, will require forethought and preparation. Speaking with the press is not a task to delegate. The community sees the **Principal** in charge of the school and responsible for the actions taken or avoided. As the visible leader of the school, the Principal must speak to the press and determine the limits of their involvement at the school. This can be achieved by submitting information about specific programs, successes and awards achieved at your school, and other human interest stories. Principals should remember that citizens have a right to know what is happening at the school.

Reporters see their role as being responsible for bringing this important information to the public. If you encounter a reporter who is either insensitive to the situation or tends to distort what you say, give that person minimal information. Do not attempt to exclude them from a story. This will make things worse. When asked questions by reporters, answer without volunteering information. You can give different levels of information.

Also, avoid the response "no comment." This tends to suggest that there may be an attempt to hide something. The "No Comment" approach will not eliminate all the difficulties you may encounter with the press during an incident (Petersen & Straub, 1992).

The Principal has a responsibility to keep all staff informed of the facts as they become available. Staff must also understand the importance of squelching rumors. No staff or faculty member is required to be interviewed by the media. If the media is attempting to interview a teacher, the Principal must obtain the teacher's permission to be interviewed, and then grant them permission to be interviewed while on school property. The Principal has the right to deny the media interviews with teachers on school property. Teachers have the right to deny an interview at any time or place. If a reporter is attempting to interview a student, the Principal must grant permission and the student must be willing to be interviewed. Parental permission should be sought. Some parents may choose not to have their children interviewed by the media.

SETTING LIMITS

Principals have the right to determine who is allowed on school property and to which areas of the school they have access. Principals are advised to use this right proactively by setting limits for the media. This means that during the initial call or contact with the media inform them as to where, when, and for how long you will meet with them. By following this procedure you will help maintain the necessary order and reduce stress to students.

In order to protect students and staff while the media is present an interview site should be chosen that is away from the main area of student activity. The meeting itself does not have to be long. It should be long enough to deliver the prepared statement followed by a short question period. At this time no teachers or students should be available for interviews and no members of the media will be admitted beyond the meeting area. When reporters arrive, have a staff member familiar with the guidelines accompany them to the meeting location and back to the front door after the meeting is over. Do not leave reporters unescorted while on school property. It is wise to clearly state all restrictions placed on the media while on school property when scheduling the first meeting. Ensure that members of the media understand and agree to these restrictions.

GUIDELINES

DEALING WITH THE MEDIA
▷ Develop a written statement for the media.
▷ Never speak to the media "off the record."
▷ Develop a message to be given over the telephone and assign people to handle the phones.
▷ Appoint spokesperson to deal with the media; this should be the **Principal**.
▷ Set time and location to meet with the media, and any follow-up meetings in advance.
▷ Appoint a staff person to escort media to and from any meeting at the school. Do not leave the media unescorted while on school property.
▷ Be proactive with press; contact the press before they contact you.
▷ State any restrictions imposed on media while on school property (no photographs, no student interviews, no teacher interviews unless approved by Principal and teacher etc.).
▷ Stress positive action taken by school; give periodic updates.
▷ Maintain confidentiality where necessary.
▷ Stress services available to students.
▷ Do not refuse to speak with the press.
▷ Announce changes made after the incident has passed.

WRITTEN STATEMENT

Prior to meeting with the media have a written statement prepared. Prepare this statement with input from your crisis team. State only the facts and avoid speculation. Once the facts have been reported, present the positive actions the school is taking to help students deal with the incident. This is also a good time to make community announcements relating to events such as the memorial service, parent meetings, and follow-up activities for students. All statements must be truthful; false statements will eventually come to the surface. A perspective that the school is attempting to cover up important facts or information will cause trouble. Do not issue disclaimers of responsibility until all facts are known. The school needs to be seen as dealing with the problem, not attempting to abdicate responsibility. The Principal should remind the media of the consequences of sensationalizing a suicide if that is the situation at hand. The Principal is the most appropriate person to prepare and issue the official statement at the school. Though the local or area superintendent oversees schools, it is the Principal who is seen by the community as being ultimately responsible for the school.

ANNOUNCEMENTS TO THE MEDIA

Examples of announcements that may be made by the Principal to the media are included below. The communications officer may make similar announcements to the media, though his/her focus should be limited to information about the departmental response to the affected school and school-based crisis team.

- ### *Example*

> *Our third-grade students were on a field trip when their school bus was involved in an accident on the Alaska Highway. Rescue is on the scene, transporting students to the hospital. Our vice-Principal is also at the scene of the accident now. We have established a special hot line for parents to call for more information. The number is _____. Our crisis team has gone into action, helping the staff and students. More information will be released as we receive it."*

Important points made in this statement are: **(1)** the preparedness of the school for incidents of this nature; **(2)** access to information for the parents; **(3)** responsible immediate action taken by a powerful school representative at the scene; **(4)** and support already provided for students at the school.

- ### *Example*

> *"A fight involving two eleventh-grade students occurred a half block from school at 7 P.M. last evening. The incident resulted in the fatal shooting of one of our students. Police are investigating and no more is known at this time. Our school's crisis plan went into action immediately following the incident and these are the actions already taken:*
> *Our crisis committee met last night. A parent hot line has been established; the number is _____.*
> *Resources have been called in to assist our recovery.*
> *Counseling for students will be provided.*
> *Review and reinforcement of our school violence policy is underway.*

Important points made in this statement include the following. **(1)** There is an expression of loss. **(2)** The incident is coupled with a statement about the violence policy thereby portraying the school as a positive force within the community. **(3)** Access to information is made available immediately for concerned parents thus demonstrating the forthrightness of the Principal and the ability of the school staff to handle emergencies.

- ***Example***

> *It is with great sadness that the staff and students of Yukon Elementary School have learned today of the death of one of our students, John Doe.*
>
> *John came to the school three years ago and was a student in the grade 6 class. He was a conscientious student who worked hard.*
>
> *Our heartfelt sympathies go out to his parents and the other members of his family at this time. He was a fine young man and will be greatly missed.*

ROLE OF PARENTS AT THE SCHOOL

During a crisis it is not unusual to have anxious parents come to the school. These are concerned parents who are worried about their child's emotional and physical well being. Some parents fear that their child may be negatively influenced by the death of a peer, especially in the case of a suicide, or that their child may not be able to cope with the death. It is important to assure these parents that their children are safe and that appropriate measures are being taken immediately to prevent further trauma due to the critical event.

When parents arrive at the school they should be taken to a predetermined location in the school where they have access to coffee/tea and, if available, light refreshments. Efforts should be made to prevent parents from wandering about the school. If parents wish to withdraw their child from the school they should not be sent to the classroom to retrieve the child, but a staff member responsible for monitoring parents should do this. When parents are at the school they should also be given an opportunity to speak with one of the crisis team members who can answer questions. Often parents do not know what to say or do after their child has been involved in or exposed to a critical incident. In response to this need, a crisis team member should schedule time after school to meet with parents. During this meeting suggestions and information should be provided to parents so they can assist their children to cope more effectively with the critical incident.

LETTER TO PARENTS

Due to the fact that many parents will have concerns about their children and their ability to deal effectively with the critical incident, an **information letter** is prepared at the school by the Principal and sent home with every child in the school. The Principal is the most appropriate and influential person to write the **information letter** to parents. The letter outlines the nature of the situation without violating confidentiality. In addition to detailing steps taken, services offered at the school for students and an acknowledgement of loss if a death is involved is part of the letter. The back of the letter lists the emotional, behavioral, and cognitive signs, as well as strategies that parents may take to help their children cope with the incident. Parents are told these signs are a normal reaction to a traumatic event. It is important to contact the parents of any students who are having a difficult time at school coping with the death.

- ## *Information Letters*

Example

May 17, 1997

Dear Parents and Guardians:

This morning we received news that the body of Tom Smith was found Wednesday evening in a rocky area near the ski hill. He has been missing since January 21, 1997. Tom had been a student at YJSS for the past three years. He was a quiet, conscientious student with a keen interest in sports. Tom was well liked by his peers and teachers.

Our school responded this morning by informing students of the sad news. We arranged for counseling within the school. Students were given the opportunity to attend a debriefing session conducted by our counselors. Students closely connected with Tom were also able to participate in a circle led by Frank McLeod and Mary Burbine and other members of the community. A counseling area has been established in the school and students with concerns have been encouraged to attend. We are pleased with the level of support offered by the community, staff, Department of Education, and fellow students.

Counseling services will continue through this week and as needed thereafter. We have also included suggestions, which you may find helpful, for assisting your child in coping with Tom's death.
If you have questions about your child's response to the news of Tom's death, please call Ms. Payne, school counselor, or Jack Andrews, Principal, at 633-0000.

Our condolences are extended to Tom's family, friends, and members of the school community as they deal with his untimely death.

Yours sincerely,

Jack Andrews
Principal

Example

Dear Parents/Guardians:

On Saturday we received news that one of our students, Jane Doe, had been involved in a fatal vehicle accident. The accident occurred on Friday evening at the Turtle Creek intersection of the Alaska Highway. We understand that there was prompt response by the police, ambulance, and medical services. Jane passed away en route to Whitehorse. She was actively involved in our student council and a member of our basketball team. Jane was a very friendly and popular student at our school, well liked by her peers and teachers. Jane will be greatly missed.

Our school responded on Sunday with the implementation of our crisis plan. Teachers were contacted and our department school psychologist arrived from Whitehorse. The school was open on Monday for student counseling and support. We were pleased with the turnout and way students were supporting one another.

Today at the school students were informed about the facts related to the accident and were provided with opportunities to discuss their feelings and strategies related to ways of coping with their loss. A counseling area has been established in the school library and students who have expressed the need to talk or receive support have been encouraged to attend. We are pleased with the level of support offered by the community, staff, Department of Education, and fellow students.

Counseling services will continue through to Thursday afternoon and as needed thereafter. Our school psychologist is expected to return to Whitehorse next Monday through Wednesday. We have also included suggestions, on the back of this letter, which you may find helpful in assisting your child in coping with Jane's death.

If you have questions about your child's response to the news of Jane's death, please call Mary Brooks or myself at 994-8000.

Our condolences are extended to the family, friends, and members of the school community as they deal with Jane's untimely death.

Yours sincerely,

Joanne Smith
Principal

There are seven important points made in both letters. These points should be included in all such letters.

1. Statement of positive characteristics of the student.

2. Immediate response by the school.

3. What students have been told about the incident.

4. Services available to students.

5. Availability of specialists at the school to answer questions from parents.

6. Expression of loss.

7. Specific information about grief and coping.

- ***Example of Reverse Side Of Letter***

<u>***Helping Children Work Through Their Grief***</u>

- Be aware of your own feelings about loss in general, and about children and death in particular.
- Help them grieve by sharing information, acknowledging reactions and feelings, and providing opportunities for expression.
- Acknowledge their pain; don't overprotect or hurry them.
- Be comfortable to sit and listen; your behavior and attitude is more important than words.
- Provide information about the grief process.
- Maintain structure and routine while allowing some flexibility for particular needs; involve children in decisions.
- Offer opportunities for rituals and times to remember the person who has died.
- If they are not talking to you, find out if they have other supports: teachers, friends, neighbors, or relatives.
- If you have questions or concerns, consult with a grief counselor, art or play therapist, or child psychologist.

<u>***Adolescent Grief***</u>

- Initial response: shock, numbness, disbelief.
- May next feel helpless and frightened; may try to "carry on."
- Feels conflict between childlike needs and adult-like expectations.
- Anger, already present in a major way in teens, is now focused towards death.
- May begin to act out feelings.
- Idealization of dead person.
- Guilt and self-blame.
- Delayed mourning.
- Clinging to mannerisms, ideas, and behaviors of the person who has died.
- Fear of renewed closeness.
- May behave in negative ways to elicit care from others.

<u>***Emergency Agencies & Telephone Numbers***</u>

- Crisis Line
- Social Worker
- Poison Control
- Physician
- Police
- Clergy

HOW PARENTS CAN HELP CHILDREN COPE

Grieving children will need continued support at home. Even though they may have talked extensively with peers, teachers, and counselors at school they will have questions and concerns that will come up while they are at home. Parents can help their children by following the suggestions listed below.

- Talk with your child and provide clear and simple answers to his/her questions.
- Talk about your own feelings.
- Listen to your child. Remember that you cannot talk and listen at the same time.

    ▷ Provide reassurance to your child that things will be all right.

    ▷ Provide physical comfort.

    ▷ Make sure that your child gets plenty of sleep, eats well, and gets exercise.

    ▷ Take the time to tuck your child in bed at night.

    ▷ If needed, repeat information and reassurances to your child.

    ▷ Make time to play with your child. This helps to relieve tension.

    ▷ If your child has a security blanket or toy, let him/her rely on it more than usual.

- ***Helpful Reactions by Parents***

    ▷ Be aware of your own feelings about loss in general, and death, in particular;

    ▷ Help them grieve by sharing information, acknowledging reactions and feelings, providing opportunities for expression;

    ▷ Acknowledge their pain; don't overprotect or hurry them;

    ▷ Be comfortable to sit and listen; your behavior and attitude are more important than words;

    ▷ Provide information about the grief process;

    ▷ Maintain structure and routine while allowing some flexibility for particular needs; involve youth in decisions;

    ▷ Offer opportunities for rituals and times to remember the person who has died;

    ▷ If they are not talking to you, find out if they have other supports: teachers, friends, neighbors, relatives;

    ▷ If you have questions or concerns, consult with the school counselor, or a counselor at a local hospice.

HELPING TEENAGERS DEAL WITH GRIEF

Listed below are suggestions that parents may find useful when helping their teenaged child or children deal with death or grief.

- ***Things To Consider About Adolescent Grief.***

    ▷ Youth at this age can understand the permanence of death and initially will respond with shock, disbelief, or numbness.

- May have difficulty concentrating; may feel helpless and frightened; may be anxious.

- May begin to act out feelings; may behave in negative ways to elicit care from others.

- May exhibit physical symptoms such as headaches; loss of appetite or overeating; rashes, and other vague pains.

- Feels conflict between child-like needs and adult-like expectations.

- Anger already present in a major way in teens, is now focused towards death.

- May feel guilt and self-blame, especially if they remember a negative interaction with the deceased individual.

- Delayed mourning is a possibility and if this symptom occurs at a later date, consider the possibility that it may be related to an earlier loss.

- Clinging to mannerisms (ideas and behaviors) of the person who has died.

- May revert to "younger" more dependent behavior.

PART 5. CRISIS COUNSELING

STUDENT DROP-IN CENTER

When a traumatic incident involving junior/senior high students develops one of the first strategies for dealing with a large number of students is to establish a **Student Drop-In Center** in the school. The center is an area in the school where students can go to receive support and help in dealing with the loss. Two or more staff members should monitor the center. The structure at the center is informal and students are encouraged to talk among themselves. The center should remain set up for two or three days. It is important not to refer to the center as a counseling center, as this may have negative connotations to some students. When establishing a center consider the following points as outlined by Qualicum School District (1997):

- ‣ Designate the library or other large classroom as the **Student Drop-In Center**.
- ‣ Ensure that all students and staff know where the center is located.
- ‣ Assign two counselors or team members to the center. They will provide support and assistance to students as needed.
- ‣ If possible have coffee, tea, or juice available.
- ‣ Encourage students to express their feelings about the loss.
- ‣ Provide an atmosphere that is non-judgmental. Remember that students need someone who is willing to listen to them.
- ‣ Review the facts of the incident and remember to point out that they are in no way responsible for what has happened, especially when the critical incident is in response to a suicide. Close friends of the victim may feel they are responsible for the death or could have prevented it. Discuss feelings of survivor guilt associated with the incident.
- ‣ Encourage students to provide mutual support to each other.
- ‣ Keep large groups of students from forming as this may contribute to hysteria. Students tend to feed off the emotions of each other. If a large group begins to form ensure that one of the counselors or crisis team members is in the group.
- ‣ Help students identify what resources they will use to cope with the situation.

> Remember to rotate staff that has been assigned to the center.

> Remind all teachers that any student may attend the center.

HALL MONITORS

Areas of the school that should be monitored include all hallways and washrooms. These are areas where students tend to gather. Students should not be left to roam about the school or gather in unsupervised areas. Due to the emotional state of some individuals they may become destructive and there is potential for damage to school property. Most often this damage is inflicted in response to the grief and anger experienced by individuals close to the victim. Other students not affected by the incident may, in fact, be influenced by the emotionality of the affected individuals in these areas of congregation. Thus it is important to appoint staff to monitor these areas.

INDIVIDUAL FUNCTIONING

During a critical incident it is important to assess an individual's overall functioning. To assess an individual's functioning one should observe and listen to the person, present problems during a discussion to determine ability to problem-solve, and evaluate general stability. Ability to make changes and deal with the world on a daily basis is vital to how the individual copes and deals with crisis-related hurtles. It is not unusual for individuals to be slightly disoriented and confused during a critical incident. During any critical incident some individuals may be either moderately or seriously impaired. Signs of moderate/severe impairment during and after the incident follow. This information has been adapted from work completed by K. Johnson (1993).

- ## *Moderately Impaired During Incident*

COGNITIVE	PHYSICAL
▷ Confusion.	▷ Headache.
▷ Difficulty solving problems.	▷ Heart palpitations.
▷ Trouble prioritizing.	▷ Muffled hearing.
▷ Time distortions.	▷ Nausea.
▷ Memory loss.	▷ Cramps.
▷ Anomie (disorientation/alienation caused by the perceived absence of social/emotional support).	▷ Profuse sweating.
	▷ Rapid breathing.
	▷ Faintness.

EMOTIONAL	BEHAVIORAL
▷ Fear.	▷ Lethargy
▷ Anxiety.	▷ Aimless wandering.
▷ Anger.	▷ Dejection.
▷ Irritability.	▷ Hysteria.
▷ Frustration.	▷ Memory problems.
	▷ Hyperactivity.

- ## *Moderately Impaired After Incident*

COGNITIVE	PHYSICAL
▷ Fear of 'going crazy'.	▷ Fatigue.
▷ Preoccupation with incident.	▷ Psychosomatic problems.
▷ Orientation toward past.	▷ Increased illness.
▷ Denial of importance of event.	▷ Physical concerns.
▷ Problems concentrating.	

EMOTIONAL	BEHAVIORAL
▷ Depression.	▷ Substance abuse.
▷ Grief.	▷ Self-destructive behavior.
▷ Numbness.	▷ Sudden lifestyle changes.
▷ Resentment/rage.	▷ Social withdrawal.
▷ Guilt.	▷ Sleep disorders.
▷ Fear of reoccurrence.	▷ Compulsive talking.
▷ Phobic reactions.	▷ Avoidance behavior.
	▷ Problems at work.
	▷ Family problems.
	▷ Flashbacks, nightmares.

It is important to remember that a crisis creates disturbances in various areas (e.g. cognition, emotion, and behavior). These disturbances should be expected and are usually transitory in nature, but when these disturbances go to an extreme they impair individual functioning. When functioning is impaired it seriously hampers the individual's ability to make rational decisions and apply a solution or problem-focused approach to dealing with the crisis. Below are signs of serious impairment during and after a critical incident.

- *Seriously Impaired During/After Incident*

COGNITION...	BECOMES
Slight disorientation.	Can't tell own name, date, or describe event.
Problems prioritizing.	Exclusive preoccupation.
Denial of severity.	Denial of incident.
Flashbacks.	Hallucinations.
Self-doubt.	Paralysis.
Numbing.	Disconnection.
Problems planning.	Lifestyle dysfunction.
Confusion, misperceptions.	Acting on bizarre beliefs.

EMOTIONS...	BECOME
Upset, crying.	Hysteria.
Anger, self-blame.	Threat to others.
Dulled response.	No response, rigidity.
Anxiety.	Fetal position.
Fatigue, slowness.	Physical shock.
	Panic.

BEHAVIOR...	BECOMES
Excessive talking, laughter.	Uncontrolled.
Restlessness, excitement.	Unfocused agitation.
Frequent retelling.	Ritualistic, continual acting.
Pacing, hand wringing.	Ritualistic behavior.
Withdrawal.	Immobility, rigidity.
Disheveled appearance.	Can't care for self.

Individuals should be referred for an immediate psychiatric assessment when there are signs and symptoms of serious impairment. This is an indication that the individual is having difficulty functioning and coping normally, and that his/her personal safety is a concern.

- ### *Factors That May Increase Vulnerability*

Crisis affects everyone differently. However, there are certain factors that can increase individual vulnerability and affect how widespread and serious the effects of a traumatic event will be. Understanding the implications of these factors will help in dealing with the crisis and the individuals. According to Petersen & Straub (1992) and Johnson (1993), the following factors may increase a student's vulnerability during a critical incident.

Critical Event Occurs Within A Closely-Knit Community

Often children come from neighborhoods where they have lived all their lives. Because of this, a critical event occurring in the life of one student could affect most of the children that live in the community.

The Critical Event Has Multiple Eyewitnesses

It is traumatic for any student to hear about the death of a peer; actually witnessing the event has a much more serious effect.

The Victim(S) Had Special Significance

When the victim had special significance within the community many students tend to identify with him/her.

The Community Is Exposed To Widespread Destruction Or Carnage

Widespread destruction or a number of deaths in a community has a profound effect on all members of the community.

Incidents That Attract A Great Deal Of Media Attention

Often the media brings stories and events into the lives of students who may otherwise see the situation as being personally remote. By doing so the event is made more real and thus more people may be drawn into the mourning.

Exposure To Prior Trauma

A recent previous suicide, death, or other loss will make the individual more vulnerable to the negative effects of the current trauma.

Family Crisis

Dysfunctional families may impair an individual's ability to cope effectively with a critical incident. Family structure and the responses taken by the family can result in successful resolution of a crisis for the individual at home or at school. Characteristics of a functional family are flexibility, affection, healthy adult relationship, healthy parent-child relationship, shared decision-making, common social activities, a healthy network of support with extended family members, and knowledge gained through previous crises and experiences. Dysfunctional families tend to be isolated within their own communities and do not exhibit the aforementioned characteristics of a healthy family.

Other Characteristics

Feelings of inadequacy and physical fatigue will increase vulnerability to trauma.

ASSESSING FAMILY SUPPORT FOR CHILDREN

School crisis response teams do not normally provide direct support and services to families that are in a crisis state; however it is possible that one of the crisis team members may deal with such a situation through the normal course of his/her work. It is helpful to determine the degree of available support for the affected individual, especially if the individual is having a great deal of difficulty coping with the crisis at school. This assessment is not meant to be an investigation into the family or to accumulate specific facts. It is possible that family support is impaired and that may be part of the problem. Thus it is important to determine the family's contributions to the existing problem and its ability to be part of the solution. When attempting to assess the level of family support consider the following points.

> Determine the composition of the current family and the basic interaction between members.

> Have there been past events within the family that could intensify coping with the current crisis?

> Determine the authority structure within the family, e.g. father, mother, grandparent etc.

> Determine how decisions are made.

> Determine who tends to provide the most emotional support.

> Are there any divisions within the family that could affect decision-making?

> Has anyone in the family experienced a traumatic event that could affect their ability to assist the individual cope with the current crisis?

> Are there any current factors affecting the family's ability to cope (e.g., illness, financial difficulties, recent move, marriage problems, etc.)?

Family impairment may be either moderate or serious. **Moderate Impairment** within the family is indicated by its inability to meet the affected individual's emotional or physical needs due to the crisis. This would place additional stress on the family. **Serious Impairment** within the family is indicated when the individual's basic needs cannot be met, or where there is potential for abuse or injury.

EFFECTS OF TRAUMA ON CHILDREN

Trauma can have both short and long-term effects on children. These effects are listed in the two tables below (Johnson, 1989):

SHORT-TERM EFFECTS OF TRAUMA
> Frozen in place: shock, disorientation, numbness.
> Fight-or-flight response: adrenaline pumps, heart races, hyperventilation occurs.
> Exhaustion: when fight-or flight can no longer be prolonged.
> Shock: disbelief, denial.
> Cataclysm of emotions: anger/rage, fear/terror, grief/sorrow confusion/self-doubt.
> Reconstruction of emotional equilibrium.

LONG-TERM EFFECTS OF TRAUMA

> Similar but milder reaction to trigger event.

> Grief due to losses.

> Flashbacks (often associated with guilt).

> Recurrent dreams and fear of sleeping.

> Repetitive play with themes of trauma.

> Avoidance of reminders.

> Amnesia.

> Loss of recently acquired skills.

> Diminished interest.

> Numbed feelings.

> Sense of foreshortened future.

> Outbursts of anger.

> Concentration impairment.

> Hyperventilation.

> Reactions at time of anniversary of event.

STAGES OF GRIEF

Dealing with grief is difficult work, both physically and emotionally. When an individual experiences a traumatic event where there is loss, that person will work through a grief process. When assisting a grieving person the goal is to: take the person beyond their initial reactions to the loss and get them to the point where they believe that they will survive. Individuals do not work through the grief process at the same rate and progression may not be linear. Remember this process takes time, effort, and determination. The stages of grief are described below:

1. Denial/Shock

> Feelings of numbness.

> Belief or feeling that deceased will return.

> Insomnia/sleeplessness.

> Loss of appetite (people literally forget to eat).

> Inconsistent behavior.

> Bargaining with God.

> Persistent dreams or nightmares.

> Inability to concentrate.

> Preoccupation without being able to identify with what.

> Confusion.

2. Fear

> Nightmares.

> Sleeplessness.

> Easily startled.

> Anxiety and restlessness.

> Verbal expression of false bravado.

> Phobias.

3. Guilt

> Often masked by anger.

> Self-destructive behavior.

> Apologetic attitude.

> Acting out in response to praise or compliments.

4. Depression (Typical)

> Lethargy.

> Decreased attention span.

> Frequent crying.

> Unkempt appearance.

> Disinterest in activities.

> Suicidal thoughts.

> Withdrawal from friends.

> Overeating or loss of appetite.

> Oversleeping or inability to sleep.

5. Depression (Masked)

> Substance abuse.

> Consistent inappropriate joking.

> Involvement in high-risk behaviors.

> Gains reputation of "party person."

> Sexual promiscuity.

> Adoption of an "I don't care" attitude.

6. <u>Reorganization</u>

> Dreams of deceased become infrequent.

> Joy and laughter return.

> Planning for the future begins.

> Reinvestment in activities once dropped or forgotten.

Other signs of grief may include feelings of sadness, guilt, anxiety, irritability, and loneliness. Physical symptoms may include: uncontrollable bouts of crying; lack of concentration; indecision; loss of appetite; nausea, sensitivity to external stimuli such as noise, light and temperature; breathlessness; sleep disturbances; physical weakness; digestive upsets, and listlessness or lack of energy. Note that individuals who react the strongest are those who were closest to the deceased. Also, individuals recovering from an earlier traumatic loss, emotional problems, or family difficulties may react strongly.

In the case of suicide, individuals who may have known about the suicide plan or been involved in a "suicide pact" are definitely "**at risk**." Young children may associate the death with ghosts and spirits. Young children often think that the situation is reversible. They may develop fear of being abandoned and worry about their parents' dying or concerned about their own death. Some young children equate death with moving away, whereas others may see death as punishment for some wrongdoing.

Adolescents tend to move between adult and child-like behaviors. When a death has occurred, they may react with unexpected emotional intensity and confusion. To avoid the reality of death they may resort to excessive denial or withdrawal.

- ## *What Grieving Individuals Need*
    1. Outside help from relatives and friends.
    2. Someone who can help them process their most frightening thoughts and feelings, which may include attacking and blaming other family members.
    3. Support of friends who attend the memorial service, and drop by or stay in touch.

4. Information about the grief process and resources they can use.

5. Access to people who are comfortable talking about loss.

6. Someone on whom they can displace their anger, pain, and frustration.

- ### *Four Goals of Grief*

Grief is a process. It is about sadness, tears, pain, anger, and loss. It is a healing process that allows us to eventually return to our normal state of daily functioning. Grief is also a process that requires active participation by the grieving individual. *Things will not return to normal by attempting to wait for things to get better.* Clayton (1994) states that grieving children are faced with certain tasks. These tasks were first defined by Sandra Fox and served as the basis for her "Good Grief Program." The four tasks as presented by Clayton are presented below:

Understand

Individuals must understand that death is universal. Everything that lives must die some day; this is not anybody's fault. Individuals must understand that the deceased does not feel anything because his/her body does not function in the same way as when he/she was alive. Finally, the individual must understand that death is *permanent*, it is *irreversible*.

Grieve

Individuals must understand there are many feelings associated with grieving. It is important that he/she is able to express and experience these feelings.

Commemorate

Grieving individuals must remember the whole life of the deceased. He/she had both good and bad things.

Move On

Once an individual has moved through the grief process it is important for him/her to get on with his/her life.

AGE SPECIFIC REACTIONS TO LOSS

A child's perception of death and his/her age must be taken into consideration when developing a crisis plan. There is considerable difference between the way a child in grade one understands and perceives death and loss compared with an adolescent in grade eight. For example, a child who is chronologically six years old but is at a developmental age of nine years, is emotionally six years old but is intellectually nine years old. He/she will have the ability to understand that death is final, but will lack the coping skills to deal effectively with the incident. The following table presents age-specific reactions to death and loss as reported by Petersen & Straub (1992):

REACTIONS TO LOSS BY AGE

1. AGE 3-5: *Often ask questions.*

  ▷ Death is seen as an ending.

  ▷ Death is not permanent, person will return.

  ▷ They fear separation and abandonment.

2. AGE 5-10: *Tend to express themselves mainly through music/art/play.*

  ▷ Reduced attention span.

  ▷ Significant changes in behavior.

  ▷ Tend to fantasize about the event.

  ▷ Mistrust of adults.

  ▷ Tend to be very concrete in their understanding.

3. AGE 10-12 girls, 12-14 boys: *Childlike in attitude.*

  ▷ Anger at unfairness of the incident.

  ▷ Excited about their survival.

  ▷ May attribute symbolic meaning to the event.

  ▷ Tend to be self-judgmental.

  ▷ May exhibit psychosomatic symptoms/illnesses.

4. AGE 13-18 girls, 15-18 boys: *Tend to respond in adult-like manner.*

  ▷ Tend to be judgmental.

  ▷ Morality crisis.

  ▷ May move toward adult responsibilities in an effort to assume control.

  ▷ Tend to be suspicious and guarded.

  ▷ May experience both sleeping and eating disorders.

  ▷ May abuse both drugs and alcohol.

  ▷ May tend to become impulsive.

THINGS TO EXPECT WHEN GRIEVING

It is important to keep in mind that when there is a death or traumatic event there are certain things that you can expect about how you may respond to grief. Listed below are a number of characteristics you may experience (Rando, 1996):

- Your grief will take longer than most people think it should.
- Your grief will take more energy than you can imagine.
- Your grief will involve continual changes.
- Your grief will show itself in all spheres of your life; social, physical, emotional, thinking, spiritual.
- Your grief will depend upon how you perceive the loss.
- You will grieve for many things (both symbolic and tangible), not just the death itself.
- You will grieve for what you have lost already as well as for the future; for the hopes, dreams, and unfulfilled expectations you held for that person.
- Your grief will involve a wide variety of feelings and reactions: some expected, some not.
- You may have some identity confusion: due to the intensity and unfamiliarity of the grieving experience and uncertainty about your new role in the world.
- You may experience a combination of anger and depression: irritability, frustration, and intolerance.
- You may feel guilt in some form.
- You may have a lack of self-concern and poor self-worth.
- You may experience spasms, waves or acute upsurges of grief that occur without warning.
- You will have trouble thinking and making decisions: poor memory and organization.
- You may feel like you are 'going crazy'.
- You may be obsessed with the death or preoccupied with thoughts of the dead person.
- You will search for meaning in/for your life and question your beliefs;

> Society has unrealistic expectations about your mourning and may respond inappropriately.

> You will have a number of physical reactions.

> Certain dates, events, seasons and reminders will bring upsurges in your grief.

> Certain experiences later in life may resurrect intense grief feelings for you.

PANIC ATTACK

An individual may experience a **Panic Attack** upon exposure to a situation that causes anxiety. These attacks usually last from a few minutes to, in rare cases, possibly hours. They are unexpected and do not occur immediately before or. In addition, the attack is not triggered by a situation whereby the individual is the focus of attention. An important feature of panic attacks is the fact that they occur unexpectedly. Over time certain situations may become associated with panic attacks. Typically panic attacks start with the onset of intense apprehension, fear, or terror. Listed below are the major symptoms of a panic attack:

SYMPTOMS OF PANIC ATTACK
> Palpitations, pounding heart or accelerated heart rate.
> Sweating.
> Trembling or shaking.
> Sensations of shortness of breath or smothering.
> Feeling of choking.
> Chest pain or discomfort.
> Nausea or abdominal distress.
> Feeling dizzy, unsteady, lightheaded, or faint.
> De-realization (feelings of unreality) depersonalization (being detached from oneself).
> Fear of losing control or going crazy.
> Fear of dying.
> Numbing or tingling sensations.
> Chills or hot flashes.

POST TRAUMATIC STRESS DISORDER

Post Traumatic Stress Disorder (PTSD) is a common human reaction that is actually *a normal response to an abnormal event.* PTSD can be devastatingly disruptive for years; in many cases however, it can be prevented.

Reactions to trauma-inducing incidents occur in three phases:

1. The **Impact** phase occurs immediately following an event and can last minutes or days. During this phase, the person is either functioning mechanically (on "automatic") or is so stunned he/she cannot act at all. Denial of the effects is common.

2. The **Recoil** phase can last a few days to several weeks. There is a great need to retell the story during this time. Individuals will also become overactive, particularly to any reminders of the event. The emotional reactions during this phase are angry outbursts, bouts of uncontrollable crying, and sometimes panic attacks can occur.

3. The **Post Traumatic Stress Disorder** phase begins weeks or even months after the event has occurred. People will feel a great sense of grief not only for whatever losses may have been sustained but also for the collapse of their assumptions and beliefs about the world. Survivor guilt is usually present, especially when a person benefits from the disaster. The destruction of assumptions (e.g., assumption of invulnerability, assumption that the world is meaningful, assumption of self-image) are often questioned during this period Johnson (1993).

SYMPTOMS OF POST TRAUMATIC STRESS DISORDER
‣ Recurrent and intrusive recollections of the event.
‣ Nightmares.
‣ Numbing of emotions.
‣ Marked disinterest in activities.
‣ Feelings of detachment.
‣ Hyper-vigilant or avoidance-behavior.
‣ Decline in cognitive performance.
‣ Startled reactions.
‣ Overwhelming and persistent guilt.
‣ Attacks of shallow breathlessness heart palpitations, sweating, shaking.

SYMPTOMS SPECIFIC TO CHILDREN
▷ Distortion of time concerning the incident.
▷ Distortion of the sequence of events.
▷ Retrospective identification of supposed premonitions.
▷ Reenactments of traumatic events (usually not conscious).
▷ Repetitive play involving traumatic themes.
▷ Pessimistic expectations of the future and life span.
▷ Marked and enduring personality changes.
▷ Greater memory of the event than adults.
▷ Fantasizing changes to "undo" the event.

POST TRAUMA SIGNS FOR ELEMENTARY STUDENTS

COGNITIVE	PHYSICAL
▷ Confusion re:	▷ Complaints (vision, stomach).
- Event.	▷ Headaches.
- Sequencing.	▷ Itching.
- Inability to concentrate.	▷ Sleep disturbances.

EMOTIONAL	BEHAVIORAL
▷ Fear of reoccurring, related event.	▷ Clinging.
▷ Wanting to be fed, dressed.	▷ Resumption of symptoms.
▷ School phobia, avoids groups.	▷ Competition with siblings.
▷ Responsibility, guilt over behavior.	▷ Repetitive talking, re-enacting events.
▷ Aggression.	▷ Disobedience.
▷ Excessive concern re family safety.	▷ Drop in school performance.
	▷ Nightmares.

POST TRAUMA SIGNS FOR JUNIOR/SENIOR HIGH STUDENTS

COGNITIVE	PHYSICAL
▷ Problems concentrating	▷ Headaches
▷ Over-concern re: health	▷ Vague complaints, pain
	▷ Skin rashes
	▷ Loss of appetite, overeating

EMOTIONAL	BEHAVIORAL
▷ Depression.	▷ Fails to meet responsibilities.
▷ Anxiety.	▷ Resumes earlier coping styles.
	▷ Withdraws socially.
	▷ Exhibits antisocial behavior.
	▷ Experiences survivor guilt.
	▷ Abuses, drugs, alcohol.
	▷ Decline in school performance.
	▷ Suddenly shifts in attitude, styles.
	▷ Acts "too old, too soon."
	▷ Drops out, pregnancy, marriage.
	▷ Makes precipitous life decisions.
	▷ Sudden changes in relationships.

PREVENTING POST TRAUMATIC STRESS DISORDER

There are a number of strategies used to reduce and/or eliminate Post Traumatic Stress Disorder in children, adolescents, and adults (Johnson, 1993). The most frequently used strategies include **defusing emotions**, **group discussions** and **debriefings** (individual and group). These procedures should be offered to both staff and students.

DEFUSING EMOTIONS

Following any violent crisis the school counselor(s) or crisis response team member should ensure that all students directly affected be given an opportunity to defuse their emotions before they go home and to attend debriefing over the next three days. They should also receive ongoing counseling if needed; have access to legal assistance if required; and protection from reminders of the incident. Attendance at both defusing and debriefing sessions should be mandatory for all students directly affected. The students/staff exposed to the tragic incident must talk with each other prior to leaving that day. **Do not defuse students who were directly affected by or witnessed the incident with any other students.** If this happens you run the risk of increasing the emotionality in the less affected students.

Defusing emotions involves ventilation of thoughts and emotions immediately following a traumatic event. It is the first step in starting to deal with the critical incident. **Defusing** is an unstructured activity that is conducted by the counselor, school psychologist, or other school based crisis team member who is familiar with the process. Following the defusing, individual and classroom debriefings are conducted. Debriefings begin the process of putting the incident and the individuals' reactions in perspective. They may be conducted either individually or in a group. Usually debriefings are implemented during the first day, or in the event that the traumatic event occurred on a weekend, the first day after the weekend. Debriefing for staff is usually scheduled for the following day after school. Debriefings include several phases which, once started, cannot be interrupted, even if they must go beyond class time.

The procedures for conducting **debriefing** are covered in detail in **PART 6**. The procedure for defusing emotions is presented below. This information has been adapted from Johnson (1993).

- *Procedure*

DEFUSING EMOTIONS
1. Provide information and include parents if they come to school.
2. Keep everyone together for some time (groups of 15-20).
3. Promote ventilation, ask:
▷ What was the worst part for you?
▷ Where were you when it happened? (Listen! Listen! Listen!).
4. Prepare students and parents for reactions of:
▷ Sleeplessness   Lack of concentration
▷ Nausea   Crying
▷ Irritability   Demanding
▷ Fear and anxiety   Nightmares
▷ Sweating   Numbness
▷ Withdrawal   Clinging
5. Let them know that they are normal.
6. Give them suggestions for coping.
7. Let them know when follow-up will be provided.

SOLUTION-FOCUSED BRIEF THERAPY (SFBT)

The use of **solution-focused brief therapy** (SFBT) offers a practical, time-sensitive intervention for a variety of school problems. More importantly solution-focused brief therapy is a positive approach to dealing with difficulties or issues that may be hard for students to overcome on their own.

In the context of crisis intervention, SFBT is an approach that, although short-term, is targeted at those individuals who are having difficulty overcoming their grief and loss as manifest through 'panic attacks' or Post-Traumatic Stress Disorder. In a school setting, its implementation may be within the realm of school counselors who have been professionally trained to engage in counselling. *Those who are not qualified to offer counselling should not attempt to use SFBT as outlined below. This description is offered for information only; to increase understanding of the positive impact that counselors can have in schools in post-crises support to students.*

Use of SFBT assumes the following. **(1)** All individuals have resources and are already doing something to try and solve their problem. **(2)** The goal of SFBT is to identify and use these resources in the student's best interest. **(3)** Change is constant, sometimes the problem will be present other times it will not. **(4)** Individuals are more likely to change if they define the goals and generate solutions that work for them. **(5)** At times change can occur quickly and **(6)** sometimes all that is needed is a small change to prompt other changes in the individual's life. The use of SFBT requires that the counselor be familiar with the necessary key skills and strategies listed below:

1. Use solution-focused language.
2. Use solution-focused questions, which help construct exceptions and potential solutions.
3. Use of future questions to present a picture of life after the problem has been solved.
4. Use of scaling questions to help define realistic goals.
5. Use of direct and indirect compliments.

6. Assign "doing" or "observation" tasks, dependent upon the individual's readiness to change.

- ***Procedure***

A guide to implementing SFBT is included here. You will note that at the top of the outline three types of clients are listed, **Visitor**, **Complainant**, and **Customer**. **Visitors** tend to be <u>more resistive</u> to change whereas **Customers** are actively <u>seeking solutions</u> to their problems. **Complainants** are only interested in complaining about things, not seeking solutions.

SOLUTION-FOCUSED COUNSELING		
☐ **Visitor**	☐ **Complainant**	☐ **Customer**

Establish Rapport

▷   Greetings.

Determine Purpose

▷   How can I help?

▷   What brings you here?

Define Problem

▷   Problem you would like to solve.

▷   How will you know this meeting has been successful?

Ideas About Goal Setting

▷   When the problem is solved what will be different?

▷   Use miracle questions.

▷   Suppose the problem is solved.

Explore Exceptions

▷   When were things a little better?

▷   Explore exceptions to the problem.

▷   Explore previous solutions.

▷   Explore pre-treatment changes.

▷   Explore ending of the problem sequence.

▷   Explore potential solution patterns.

▷   Amplify miracle questions.

▷   Explore coping questions.

Normalize-Validate

▷   It's been tough.

Think Break

▷   Write down what impressed you about the individual.

▷   Use client key phrases and words.

> Put together suggestions to share with client.

Share Ideas

> Summarize what impresses you.

> Validate his/her struggle to solve the problem.

> Suggest strategies to try.

Tasks

> If it works, do more of it.

> If not working do something different.

> Amplify exceptions.

> Use observation tasks.

> Do something different.

> Pretend.

> Coin toss.

> Surprise task.

Scaling Questions

> Client investment in change.

> Client confidence in change.

> Progress.

> Goal setting.

> What needs to happen to move you up one notch.

Goal Setting

> Small goals.

> Specific and concrete.

> Presence of something.

> Build on solution pattern.

> Realistic and achievable.

> Perceived as hard work.

Client Language

> Use client's language.

> State problem in past tense.

> Open possibilities through re-framing.

PART 6. GUIDELINES FOR CRISIS DEBRIEFING

CLASSROOM DEBRIEFING MODEL

If a critical incident affects a substantial number of individuals, it is preferable to conduct classroom debriefings (critical incident stress debriefings). *However, there are a number of exceptions to this guideline.* The exceptions are listed below.

- *Exceptions*
    1. The individual student shows signs of being seriously impaired due to the crisis (See Part 5).
    2. The class as a whole is not supportive of one another.
    3. The students' needs vary widely.
    4. The class is highly polarized on the issues.
    5. Involved families are highly affected by the event.
    6. **Students who were directly affected by, or witnessed the incident should not be debriefed with any other students.** To do so you run the risk of increasing the emotionality in the less affected students. For these students, debriefing should be done privately. Adolescents, in particular, tend to 'feed' off the emotions of each other.

Classroom debriefings are simply structured group discussions, *not* psychotherapy. They allow the class, as a group, to sort out the facts leading to the incident and express their reactions to it. The classroom debriefing provides a format that enables the crisis team member to put the incident and individuals' reactions in perspective, as well as clarifying any misinformation. Debriefings also attempt to salvage group cohesiveness from the disintegrating effects of a crisis. Classroom debriefings are usually implemented on the same day as the incident or a day later. Classroom debriefings can be conducted with all grades except Kindergarten and perhaps, Grade 1. At the lower elementary school level they tend to be shorter in length and are not as emotional as the junior/senior grades may be. Helpers are reminded not to present graphic details about how a victim died. Likewise, if a child asks for specific details state only how the individual died and move on to another question.

A useful strategy when conducting classroom debriefings is to assign a staff member (e.g., the classroom teacher) to assist the school-based crisis team member. A staff member can provide the necessary background information about students in the class who may be experiencing other traumatic events or outcomes from a dysfunctional family. This staff member can also be of considerable help in identifying those students "at risk." When the Principal has requested support from the District/Division, or a crisis team member has been dispatched to the school for political purposes or due to policy/procedures, that individual may assist the school-based crisis member when conducting debriefings. When conducting a classroom debriefing, have the students form a large circle. They may be seated on the floor or at their desks. A few basic ground rules when conducting a classroom debriefing are provided below. The information and model for conducting classroom debriefings presented in the table below has been adapted from, Mitchell & Everly (1993).

1. Have all students form a circle, either seated or on the floor.

2. Have an object, e.g. feather, stick, special rock, or some other object, that can be used to identify the current speaker.

3. Have a box of tissue readily at hand.

4. No family members are present in the class.

5. Clearly state the ground rules

• *__Procedure__*

CLASSROOM DEBRIEFING
1. INTRODUCTORY PHASE
The leader lays down the basic rules for participation.
▹ Introduction and purpose
▹ Confidentiality (what's said in here stays in here); no notes, taping, recording.
▹ No interrupting; No put-downs; No blaming of anyone.
▹ Speak only for yourself. Pass if you do not want to speak.
▹ Everyone is equal
2. FACT PHASE
Here students explore and gain concurrence on the sequence of events, and role each played in the incident.
▹ What happened?
▹ Who was involved?
▹ When it happened?
▹ Where it happened?
▹ How it happened?
3.THOUGHT PHASE
▹ First thing you thought about.
4. REACTION PHASE

> ▷ Worst thing about incident.
> ▷ Your first reaction.
> ▷ How are you reacting now?
> ▷ What effect has this had on you?

5. SYMPTOM PHASE
Each student is given the opportunity to share.
> ▷ What unusual things did you experience at the time?
> ▷ What unusual things are you experiencing now?
> ▷ Has your life changed in any way at home and school?

6. TEACHING PHASE
The leader provides information to the students regarding normal reactions to the incident, and anticipates later reactions. Any misconceptions regarding the incident or its effects can be cleared up.
> ▷ You are 100% normal if you have any of these **feelings**, **thoughts**, and **symptoms**- denial, avoidance, sleep difficulties, irritability, fatigue, restlessness, depression/mood swings, difficulty concentrating, nightmares, vomiting/diarrhea, suspiciousness.
> ▷ How have you coped with difficulties before?
> ▷ What are you doing to cope now?
> ▷ How will you know that things are getting better for you?

7. CLOSURE PHASE
> ▷ Remind students of strengths.
> ▷ Reassure them that it will take time to heal.
> ▷ Reassure them that you will be there.
> ▷ Any other questions?
> ▷ Want to add something?

INDIVIDUAL DEBRIEFING

Individual debriefing is a more effective method for dealing with students who are close to the victim or are having difficulty putting the critical incident into perspective. Following any crisis the school counselor(s) or crisis team member should ensure that all students directly affected attend a debriefing session over the next two days and receive ongoing counseling if needed. Attendance at debriefing sessions should be mandatory for all students directly affected. Information in the table below has been adapted from Johnson (1993).

- *Procedure*

INDIVIDUAL DEBRIEFING
1. FIND PRIVACY
Attempt to find a comfortable, private place for the conference. If the conference is to be individual, it must be private in order to engage trust. **Avoid** placing yourself in what may be perceived as a compromising position, particularly if you are male, with a female student. Stay **visible** to others.
2. MAINTAIN CALM
In all probability, the student is experiencing uncertainty and self-doubt. Presenting a balanced demeanor tells the student that what he/she is about to say will be accepted.

3. BE HONEST WITH YOURSELF

Keep in touch with your own feelings and reactions to the student, the issues, and the situation. If you feel you cannot handle the situation, ask someone else to take over, and arrange a transition.

4. READ BETWEEN THE LINES

Watch the student's behavior. Be aware of subtle messages. Draw inferences for further exploration.

5. VALIDATE FEELINGS

Feelings are neither right nor wrong. Whatever the feelings the student is experiencing, validate them. Often feelings clamor for expression; help the student clarify them.

6. LISTEN WELL

Good listening involves several skills. Use gentle probes for clarification and elaboration. Maintain good eye contact. Use increasingly focused questions when appropriate (especially when you suspect the individual capable of self-destructive behavior). Trust your hunches and check them out.

7. SHOW BELIEF

Your job at this point is to listen and to facilitate expression. You are not a judge, jury, or investigator. Show confidence, trust, and faith that what the students is saying is the truth as he/she believes it to be.

8. DISPEL FAULT

If the student was victimized let him/her know that the incident was not his/her fault. Be proactive about this, because victims tend to distrust themselves and/or others and blame themselves. Assure them that as individuals, they were not responsible for the incident. If the incident is due to a suicide, dispel any feelings that the he/she could have prevented it.

9. EXPLORE FEARS

Individuals can often tell about what happened to them, but may be unable to express assumptions they have made, questions they have, or fears they may hold about the incident. Facilitating the expression of these assumptions, questions, and fears at this point empowers the individuals to deal with them.

10. PROVIDE INFORMATION

The right information at the right time can be very helpful. If you know something about the incident, normal reactions to that type of incident, or actions that could be taken, consider sharing it; be sure not to preach and that your own need to "do something" is not clouding your judgment regarding the timeliness of the information.

11. WALK THROUGH THE PROCESS

Many processes are predictable, given a particular situation. Loss of a significant person will predictably involve the grief process. Disclosure of crime or victimization will predictably involve the police and legal procedures. When the time is right, sharing what you know about certain procedures that can assist the student in predicting and planning for his/her near future.

12. EXPLORE RESOURCES

As soon as possible, explore with the student what resources he/she has available, and what his/her support system provides. Assist him/her in deciding to whom, when, and how to 'reach out' for that support.

GROUP DEBRIEFING

Following a critical incident, students need a chance to talk about it; they do not, however, need to be coerced. Group debriefing is a useful format in which students can state their feelings about the incident in a less formal setting. Make sure every student is asked questions at each step of the process, but set a rule that at any time anyone can say "pass" and not answer. Group debriefing tends to be somewhat more structured than defusing sessions. They are usually implemented the second or third day after the incident and can signify some movement towards resolution.

- *Procedure*

GROUP DEBRIEFING

1. GROUND RULES

Ground rules can vary from group to group, but some will remain the same. Here are a few of the standard ground rules to follow.

- Confidentiality (what's said in here stays in here).
- No put-downs.
- No interrupting.
- Speak only for yourself.

2. FORMAT

A good way to handle discussing facts and feelings is to first go around the room asking individuals what they **saw** and when they became aware of the incident. Later go around asking what individuals **heard**. Finally, ask what they **felt**. This pattern establishes the principle of sharing, while it moves from cognitive to affective material.

3. NEEDS

Students may need to talk about similar incidents both current and past. This is all part of the sorting out process, and may occupy the majority of the time allotted.

4. REACTIONS

Student's emotional reactions can vary widely. They can range from unaffected or amused, to being quite shaken. An unaffected reaction, however, may be numbness.

General amusement is often a defense against anxiety. Such students may need to be protected from others seeking to displace anger.

5. WHEN IT'S OVER

Keep the discussion gently focused until it has gone its normal routine. Expect students to refer to the event and to return to discussing it in the future.

6. ASSESS

Whether students need further support (that is, if individuals are uncontrollable or seem to be in shock), and refer to the office or to whatever back up is available right away.

INTERACTIONS TO AVOID

False Promises

Don't say things you are not really sure of, or are not true. If you are unsure of something, tell them "I'm not sure, but I will find out for you." Do not say, "Everything is going to be all right!" unless you have some way of knowing that for certain.

Falling Apart

It's all right to shed some tears in empathy with another person, but it is essential to remain in emotional control. Don't fall apart or react with excessive emotion, because that sends the message that you can't be trusted with the information. The student has enough to cope with; he or she does not need to be forced to take care of your emotional problems as well.

Casting Judgments

Facial expression, body language, inferences, and questions can each communicate judgments. Even, "Why did you take so long to come to me?" signals an implied judgment, which can be more than a traumatized student can handle. Focus on the person, not upon what's right.

Inquisition

Don't play detective, searching for information to hang the perpetrator. Such inquisition will only drive the student away or make things worse. Instead, assist the student in revealing what he or she feels is necessary.

Comments

Avoid using such comments as "gone to sleep", if you need anything," or "I know you must have so many feelings now." These general statements suggest insincerity.

FACTORS THAT CAN AFFECT YOUR REACTION

There are a number of factors as indicated by Petersen & Straub (1992), that can potentially effect a crisis team member's ability to respond effectively to individuals and a critical incident. They are presented below:

- ***Common Factors***
  - ▷ Prior suicide in family.
  - ▷ Unresolved feelings of grief.
  - ▷ Marital or relationship problems.
  - ▷ Financial difficulties.
  - ▷ Personal health problems.
  - ▷ Fatigue.
  - ▷ Loss of or lack of positive feelings towards victim.
  - ▷ Isolation and withdrawal.
  - ▷ A history of, and current, personal anxiety.
  - ▷ Rigidity in thinking and resistance to change.
  - ▷ Suspicion and paranoia.
  - ▷ Fear that it will not get better.
  - ▷ Fear of losing control.

- ***Associated Factors***
  - ▷ **Fear Over Liability:** Many professionals facing crisis intervention situations suddenly become aware of their professional vulnerability. Specific fears over professional responsibilities and legal liabilities are legitimately raised.
  - ▷ **Fear Over Liability:** Commonly, professionals feel guilt at not seeing the signs of a crisis sooner or of not acting sooner than they did. Of all professional groups, teachers seem to be the most prone to guilt.

- **Inadequacies:** When confronted with catastrophic situations, staff members often feel that they can do little to "fix the pain." The expectation that "I should be able to fix it", leads to feelings of helplessness.

- **Anger:** Feelings of anger and rage are often the result of dealing with children who have been victimized by adults.

- **Desire To Protect:** Listening to the pain and unfortunate situations often creates a desire to provide 100% protection for the child, 100% of the time. Obviously this cannot be, and usually the damage has already occurred. This creates further frustration.

- **Distrust:** Distrust of the home situation, the law enforcement system, and the crisis intervention team is natural. The distrust is fueled by the "What-ifs." What if the perpetrator gets out? What if the police can't catch him or her? What if he or she gets a light sentence? What if the parents take it out on the child? What if?

- **Old Personal Issues:** Often the student's critical incident or life situation parallels your own past or present. While this can create shared experience, rapport, and understanding, it can also create discomfort, pain, and significant distraction. The adult's unfinished business can interfere with his/her focus on the student and can drain needed energy.

- **Post Crisis Vulnerability:** Extensive involvement, unfinished business, or the intensity of the situation can leave the adult in great emotional turmoil. A sense of emptiness and self-doubt later may prevail. At this time one should find a support person for help.

SELF CARE

Handling a crisis that involves students is draining and difficult. During a crisis, routines are disrupted, different management skills are called for, and emotions are subjected to a roller-coaster ride. The level of stress is compounded by the fact that student crises are rarely "fixable." Usually, there are no clear resolutions and there are no clear criteria of what is or is not successful intervention. Only with experience can professionals walk away from an intervention feeling, "Yes, that worked well," or "No, that really did not work out." There are no standards, no norms, and no evaluation system to tell us how we have done.

Stress works in an interactive cycle, with reaction to stressful situations compounding the situation itself, creating more stress. ***Stress management involves long range planning, focusing upon our expectations, our manner of interpreting situations, and evaluating the way our behaviors make situations worse.***

In the short term, it is useful to have several brief stress-breaking techniques available to use for yourself. A useful strategy is to plan time slots of five to ten minutes during the day when you can be by yourself. Use a relaxation technique prior to going home such as, brief meditation, self-hypnosis, or a stress reduction tape. Share your reaction to the incident with someone else.

Everyone manifests stress differently, but there are four general areas of impact: **physical, psychological, family,** and **work.** The type of impact can provide clues for working out an effective stress management plan. In an attempt to reduce the effects of post-traumatic stress in staff, it is important to take care of your own needs **before, during**, and **after** the critical incident has passed (Johnson, 1993).

- ***Taking Care Before A Critical Incident***
  - ⊳ Increase your knowledge and skills.
  - ⊳ Be aware of your own 'hot spots' and personal triggers.
  - ⊳ Be aware of your needs and the amount of stress you can handle.
  - ⊳ Accumulate background information.
- ***Taking Care During A Critical Incident***
  - ⊳ Don't ignore your own feelings and personal needs.
  - ⊳ Set limits for yourself.
  - ⊳ Don't drink excessive amounts of caffeine and/or alcohol.
  - ⊳ Remain constantly aware of your feelings.
  - ⊳ Exercise vigorously within twenty-four hours, if medically approved. This will

burn off any excess chemicals in the body caused by stress.

> Retain a safe distance from issues.

> Eat balanced meals and get plenty of sleep.

> Talk about the incident with your spouse, friends, and colleagues.

> Seek out help when you are in need.

- *__Taking Care After A Critical Incident__*

> Reflect upon the incident and your reactions by yourself and with support persons.

> Debrief with colleagues when necessary.

> Talk about your feelings and reactions to the incident at home.

MULTICULTURAL AWARENESS

When responding to a critical incident, you may be faced with children who are part of a different culture. To work effectively with these children consider the following points:

> Be aware of your own cultural biases and beliefs.

> Always seek clarification if you do not understand what an individual has said.

> Don't assume that you know or understand what an individual's nonverbal communication means unless you are familiar with his/her culture.

> Be aware of any of your own nonverbal communication that may be perceived as insulting in other cultures.

> Don't impose your personal values. Remain objective.

> Do not judge others from different cultures by your own cultural values.

> Get to know as much as possible about the culture.

> Remember that your lack of familiarity with a specific culture may increase the stress during the intervention.

> Remember that you can not change a person's cultural perspective.

> Continually attempt to increase your awareness of your personal preconceptions and stereotypes of the cultures with which you may be working.

FIRST NATIONS TRADITIONS

In some First Nations the **healing circle** is used in response to a critical incident.

During a **healing circle** a feather, stick, or some other object used to identify the current speaker is passed around the circle. Only the person holding the object is permitted to speak. Interruptions are not allowed when the individual holding the object is speaking, as it is considered rude and inappropriate. Once the circle has been formed, outsiders should not attempt to arbitrarily jump in without being accepted or welcomed into the group. Wait to be invited into the group. This particular procedure is easy to implement and has been used by some First Nations for hundreds of years. Using a healing circle works well when conducting a classroom debriefing. The procedure is outlined below.

- ## *Healing Circle*

HEALING CIRCLE
1. Students are first asked to form a circle, seated either on chairs or the floor.
2. The group is then introduced to the procedure. The format is similar to the classroom debriefing.
3. Once the group has moved through the introduction and fact phases, the talking feather, stone, or stick is given to one individual to start the process. If the individual does not wish to speak the object is passed to the person next to him or her.
4. Interruptions are strictly prohibited. It is most important not to interrupt the individual who has possession of the talking stone or feather.
5. Once a healing circle has been formed, outsiders should not attempt to join the circle unless invited.
6. When a healing circle is used it is most important to respect the process and those individuals involved in it.

PART 7. THE MEMORIAL SERVICE

ROLE OF THE SCHOOL

It is important that there be a helpful and appropriate response when there is a death in the school, whether it is due to accident, natural causes, or suicide. Often in small communities the school is the focal point of attention. The school not only functions as an educational facility for the children, but as a recreational center for the community. After a traumatic event has occurred in which there was a death, the principal must decide as to the appropriate response by the school.

HOW TO RESPOND

How the individual or individuals died will, in part, determine the type of response by the school. If an individual died as a result of suicide, the more appropriate response should be 'low key'. An elaborate or high profile response may draw unwanted attention to the way in which the individual died. When suicide is the cause of death, there is the fear of copycat deaths or pacts between close friends of the deceased. Any attempts to glorify the way in which the individual died should be discouraged. Glorification of suicide may inadvertently be accomplished by holding a large memorial service at the school, students establishing a shrine at the deceased student's desk or locker, or by drawing undo attention to the way the individual died. Regardless, most students will want to hold some form of memorial service for the deceased.

Remember that a school memorial service is not a substitute for the actual funeral service. The school service is a time for accepting and grieving the loss of one of its members. It is an opportunity to say, "goodbye." The service should be short. Hold the service at a time that is least likely to cause disruption in the school routine. A good time to schedule the school service is either at the beginning or end of the day, especially at the start of a weekend (Friday afternoon). This provides a natural break from school. Students will be at home for two days or more where they can receive support and comfort from parents rather than being continually exposed to and 'feeding' off the emotionality of others.

It is most important to discuss the proposed school memorial service with the family of the deceased and invite them to the service. Encourage peers and family members to participate in the service. Be aware of the deceased person's religion and, if appropriate, discuss the service with the deceased person's priest, minister, rabbi, imam, or religious leader. Make separate arrangements for those who do want to attend the service. Before holding the service it is important to determine the potential numbers of people attending so that proper accommodations are arranged. If the weather permits, the service may be held outdoors. To help keep track of the process and to organize a memorial service at the school, completing the **Memorial Service Record** located in **Appendix 4** may be helpful.

PREPARING STUDENTS

It is important for teachers to prepare their students for what to expect at a memorial service. Many young people have never been to a funeral service; thus, discussing the memorial and the activities will go a long way in reducing the anxiety and fear they may have. Students should know what to expect and what to say during the service. Knowing what to say and do during a memorial of a student with a unique ethnic or religious background may be particularly important.

After the memorial it is important to gather the students and take them back to their classrooms to give them an opportunity to discuss their feelings and reactions. Time is needed for comfort and direction. This time will help students bring closure to the incident.

It is important to involve those students closest to the deceased individual in the planning of activities and the actual memorial service. This will help bring a sense of closure to the critical incident. An effective way to resolve grief is to actively participate in the commemoration of a death. In addition, many students will want to send cards and letters to the grieving family. Others will want to create a tribute from the class.

- ### *Classroom Activities*

Listed below are a number of constructive, participatory, classroom activities that facilitate the resolution of a critical incident. These activities involve one or more students. It is important that any activity be in good taste and not go against known wishes and beliefs of the family. Participation in an activity is a positive way in which to remember the deceased and to help bring closure to the incident (Greenstone & Leviton, 1993).

> - Have the class write a poem.
> - Make a special card or other item for the parents.
> - Draw a picture of the student.
> - Write a letter to the parents.
> - Send flowers to the family.
> - Send a basket of fruit to the family.
> - Write a song about the deceased.
> - Plant a tree.
> - Attend the funeral service.
> - Name a trophy after the person.
> - Set up a bulletin board in their memory.
> - Make a garden.
> - Collect donations for the family.
> - Place a dedication in the yearbook.
> - Display a special picture, painting or sculpture as a memorial to the student.

PART 8. THE AFTERMATH

WORKING WITH TRAUMATIZED STAFF

Some staff members may develop an **Acute Stress Response (ASR)** to the critical incident. Symptoms of **ASR** are feeling overworked, frequent crying, withdrawal, lack of interest in social events, and reduced exercise. However, some staff members may remain unusually quiet. These individuals may be experiencing signs of depression. For some of these individuals, all that may be needed is rest, refreshment, and possibly a rotation to a less critical assignment. Those who have a more serious reaction to the incident may need to be placed on a light duty assignment or be allowed to return home for a period of recovery. Remember that when talking with traumatized staff, the individual may be in shock or feeling vulnerable. When individuals are in this state they need an understanding authority figure that can convince them that things are under control. If they need to cry allow them to do so. Any staff member who shows signs of **ASR** should be referred for counseling with trained personnel (Johnson ,1993). This may result in a referral to an **Employee Assistance Program** (EAP) counselor. Information about the EAP program should be made available to all staff.

It is important to counsel the Principal to expect and tolerate staff reactions to the incident, so long as they do not interfere with the students and the rest of the staff. It is wise for the Principal to schedule a debriefing for all staff members. The procedure to follow for debriefing staff is similar to the format used for classroom debriefings. After the incident, staff members should not be told what or how to feel. Remember that feelings are neither right nor wrong but they are real. This is also a time to avoid a critique of staff performance, other than to acknowledge a job well done. The following points will help to reduce some of the accumulated stress that staff experience during a critical incident:

➢ Share factual information about expected reactions, and alert staff to the potential for delayed responses to the incident.

> Explore support systems and suggest sources for additional help. This helps the individual utilize existing support and provides direction.

> Let staff members know you will continue to be available to them.

- ### *Personal Hot Spots*

Past events similar to the current incident tend to remind us of our own weaknesses and issues that we may have been trying to avoid. These **hot spots** may cause us to focus on one issue and not on others. Consequently, we may make bad judgments and ignore other pressing issues. These hot spots will also increase our stress and vulnerability to trauma. Often we are not aware of our own hot spots. When we are aware of our hot spots we are in a better position to remove ourselves from the situation. When we are not aware, we will become alerted to our vulnerability by our emotional and physical reactions. It is important for team members be aware of their own reactions because they can indicate other unresolved issues and conflicts or difficulty dealing with the current incident. Listed below is a table indicating feelings and possible implications that may be experienced by a crisis team member.

- ### *Feelings and Implications*

FEELINGS	IMPLICATIONS
> Anxiousness	> Avoiding something, fatigue
> Distraction	> Picking up on nonverbal message
> Coldness	> Over identification with incident
> Physical discomfort	> Unfinished personal business
> Sense of being overwhelmed	> Manipulation of individuals

The time to help students and staff put a crisis in perspective occurs when the incident is over and emotional and physical exhaustion have set in. Now there will be time for the affected individuals to:

> Search for meaning in the event.

> Understand and accept their emotional reactions.

> Increase their ability to cope with future adversities.

During this time you can also do the following:

> Promote maturity and growth in the students and staff.

> Integrate the emotional investment of the students into a loyalty towards their school.

> Refine and/or revise your crisis response plan.

VICARIOUS TRAUMA

Helpers working with traumatized individuals are, to some degree, likely to become traumatized as well. Conducting individual and classroom debriefings, as well as being continually exposed to the emotional responses of people reacting to a critical incident is difficult and painful. **Vicarious trauma** may not warrant clinical intervention, but it can make life miserable until the incident passes. The most obvious risk to individuals who work with grief-stricken, depressed, or suicidal individuals is that they can end up exhibiting many of the same symptoms (Johnson 1993).

- ## *Signs of Vicarious Trauma*
    > Anxious.

    > Depressed.

    > Distrustful.

    > Irritable.

    > Ineffective.

    > Suspicious.

    > Pessimistic.

    > Alienated.

- ## *Individual Receptivity*
Crisis team members should understand that it is impossible for them to attempt to remain unmoved by the incident. They remain less affected if they are able to psychologically distance themselves from the incident and engage in self-care in the evenings. Psychological distancing refers to the level of **individual receptivity** or

manner in which the helper responds to an individual needing support. This degree of receptivity can indicate how effective or ineffective the helper may be. Listed below are the different levels of receptivity as identified by Johnson (1993):

- ᐳ Absence.
- ᐳ Confused.
- ᐳ Identifies.
- ᐳ Distance.
- ᐳ Sympathetic.
- ᐳ Objectivity.
- ᐳ Empathetic.

The two most destructive psychological characteristics that a crisis response member may exhibit are **absence** and **confusion**. In the former, the victim learns that he or she is not worth the energy or effort it would take to listen to. In the latter the crisis response member confuses and disorients the victim. A team member exhibiting the characteristic of **distance** may not provide the victim with the necessary validation and support, whereas the characteristic of **identification** may mean that the victim does not receive a balanced perspective. The most effective characteristics a team member may exhibit are **objectivity**, **empathy**, and **sympathy**. If team members are going to be effective, they must develop a sense of their own receptivity and what is comfortable for them.

DEBRIEFING SCHOOL STAFF

In the aftermath of a crisis, you must debrief school staff. It is also important to include all support personnel such as secretaries and custodians. Within the first three days, usually the second or third day the principal should schedule time for staff members to attend a debriefing. This can be co-facilitated by both the counselor/school psychologist and the principal. Attendance at the debriefing should be strongly encouraged. The procedure used to debrief school staff is the **Classroom Debriefing** model presented earlier. Teachers should be asked about their reactions to the events of the day and for their input for improvement. The discussion should end with ways to take care of oneself, with participants encouraged to commit to doing one nice thing for themselves (going for a back massage, buying a special treat, going out for a nice meal at a favorite restaurant etc.) that day.

DEBRIEFING SCHOOL/DISTRICT/DIVISION CRISIS TEAMS

In the aftermath of a crisis School Based and District/Division crisis teams must be debriefed. Debriefing at this level tends to follow an **Operational Debriefing** format. This format is followed because both teams are concerned with improving their overall performance.

However, it is important to note that there may be a difference of opinion between school-based team members and district/division crisis members as to how the school responded. There may be questions about the level of district/division support; who should have been in charge of the school-based crisis team; and what actions should have taken place. School-based team members may be in an emotionally fragile state. Criticism and condemnation from district/department personnel can have a particularly destructive effect on the school-based crisis team. It is best if school-based and department crisis teams conduct independent debriefings. The **Operational Debriefing** format is suggested for both school and department crisis teams.

- *Procedure*

OPERATIONAL DEBRIEFING
1. INTRODUCTION
▷   State purpose of the debriefing.
▷   State ground rules.
2. FACTS OF THE INCIDENT
▷   Participants gain consensus on what happened.
▷   Participants gain consensus on the order things happened.
▷   The role of each team member.
3. ASSESSMENT OF THE INTERVENTION
▷   Review of team performance.
▷   Things done well.
▷   Areas for improvement.

4. REACTIONS

- ▷ Individual reaction during the incident.

5. INTERPRETATION OF RESPONSE

- ▷ Opportunity to make sense of the incident from a professional perspective.
- ▷ Chance to understand the incident.

6. PLANS FOR IMPROVEMENT

- ▷ Lessons learned for future crisis response.

7. CLOSING

- ▷ Plans to implement the lessons learned from the current incident.

ONGOING STUDENT COUNSELING

Most of the work in the aftermath of a crisis will fall upon the shoulders of the school's counselor. Invite anyone who wishes to participate for one or two groups (6-8 students each) of counseling and discussion about the incident. Students who are particularly at risk due to the crisis should be referred to the group. A few students may also require individual sessions if their problems are different from those of the other students or if they are so upset that group participation will intensify the reactions of the other members.

EVALUATING THE CRISIS RESPONSE PLAN

Once the crisis is over and things have returned to normal, it is important to evaluate the crisis response plan. If you do not conduct an evaluation you will not know if the plan was successful or if it made a difference. Evaluating the crisis plan on an annual basis will provide a degree of quality assurance to the plan. When evaluating the plan ask such questions as:

- ▷ Was the plan effective? Why? Why not?
- ▷ Was responsibility evenly distributed?
- ▷ Was there any effect on staff members who have traumatic events in their past?
- ▷ Was additional support requested from the District/Division? Why? Why not?
- ▷ Did the incident require crisis intervention or emergency support?

> ▷ What parts of the plan worked smoothly? Why?

> ▷ Which parts of the plan did not work well? Why?

> ▷ What needs to be changed for the next time?

There are *three* sources of information you can access when evaluate the crisis intervention plan. The following may be helpful in guiding your information gathering.

1. Gathering Feedback From Students

> ▷ Did the plan help them in dealing with the incident?

> ▷ Did they learn alternative strategies for dealing with the incident?

2. Gathering Feedback From The Community

> ▷ Children coping with the incident?

> ▷ Were children willing to talk about the incident to parents?

> ▷ Were parents aware that swift and positive action was being taken by the school to deal with the incident?

3. Gathering Feedback From All School Staff

> ▷ How did they feel about their responsibility?

> ▷ Were they able to handle it?

> ▷ What would they like to see changed in the plan?

> ▷ How can the plan be improved?

PART 9. RESPONSE TO SPECIFIC CRISES

SUICIDE .

Suicide is not triggered by the mere mention of the word and preparation for response to a suicide does not denote expectation of a suicide. A willingness to deal openly with issues related to suicide along with planning appropriate help and support, aims at preventing and minimizing its devastating consequences. Suicide risk factors include a sense of not belonging in a school, a sense of having a restricted future because of doing poorly in school, alienation from peers, and a low level of family support. Environmental factors in the school that may increase the risk of suicide include recent transitions imposed by the system, lack of specialized programs, a social climate with strong cliques and factions, alienation and rejection of certain students, and excess attention given to suicide threats or attempts.

A program that focuses on prevention should seek to help teachers and counselors identify the broad spectrum of "at risk" students. Curriculum on prevention should focus on development of coping skills, identification of depression, coping with depression, problem-solving techniques, decision-making strategies, and stress management.

- ### *Pre-Suicide*

At times a crisis team member may be called upon to intervene with a student or group of students identified as "at risk" for suicide. Assessing each individual is critical. Consult with those who initially identified the individual "at risk" to gather background information and social history, identify family members, situational factors, and any behavioral signs such as those listed below. Keep in mind that there is no right or wrong way to intervene with a suicidal individual. Remember that your assessment will provide an estimate of the degree of risk only. Interpretation of that risk should be made very conservatively (e.g., err on the side of suicide potential). Listed below are the common warning signs associated with suicide.

- ## *Warning Signs of Potential Suicide*

WARNING SIGNS

1. The person is preoccupied with the thoughts of death, and exhibits the following signs:

- ▷ A specific plan for a suicide attempt;
- ▷ The means of carrying out the suicide act;
- ▷ Suicide threats, notes or repeated statements about his/her death;
- ▷ Previous suicide attempt;
- ▷ Death of a significant person through suicide;
- ▷ Making final arrangements, e.g. giving favored things away, writing will, putting relationship in order; and/or,
- ▷ Sudden apparent resolution of difficulties manifests as calmness, indicating suicide as a solution.

2. The person has experienced significant (possibly recent) changes in relationships and environment:

- ▷ Loss of significant person through death, divorce, or separation;
- ▷ Loss of an object of affection;
- ▷ Loss of employment, of financial security, of status;
- ▷ Loss of health, in the form of serious illness or chronic pain; and/or,
- ▷ Geographical move or school change.

3. The person exhibits observable changes in motivation and behavior:

- ▷ Decreased work or academic performance;
- ▷ Persistent lateness or unexplained absences from work or school;
- ▷ Decreased social activity, isolation, aloofness, withdrawal;
- ▷ Apparent loss of involvement in interests and hobbies;
- ▷ Aggressiveness, moodiness, lethargy, not communicating;
- ▷ Evidence of anxiousness, extreme tension, agitation, restlessness;
- ▷ Lack of concentration, preoccupation;
- ▷ Outbursts of anger at self and/or the world;
- ▷ Self-abuse;
- ▷ Physical mutilation or other self-inflicted injury;
- ▷ Taking unwarranted risks; and/or,
- ▷ Substance abuse.

4. The person shows observable changes in affect or personality:

- ▷ Self-dislike - "I hate myself." "I'm no good;"
- ▷ Feeling hopeless and helpless;
- ▷ Feeling misunderstood and unappreciated;
- ▷ Signs of severe mental depression;
- ▷ Cries easily;

> Communication that life is too painful or difficult; and/or,
> Loss of pleasure.

5. The person exhibits physical/somatic changes:

> Loss of or increase in appetite; weight change;
> Increase or decrease in sleep;
> Exhaustion;
> Loss of physical or mental energy; and/or.
> Inability to experience pleasure.

6. Stress.

> Due to personal loss; and/or
> Sexual assault or abuse.

When dealing with an individual who may be suicidal it is most important to determine the level of risk that person presents in terms of actually attempting suicide. If you ask directly, you will know whether the person has thoughts about suicide. There are three factors used as predictors of the immediate risk of suicide. The factors are: **(1) prior** suicidal behavior; **(2)**, **current** plan, and **(3) resources** available. Remember to take all threats seriously. Ramsay, Tanney, Tierney, & Lang (1994), developed the information and format for determining level of risk.

- ### *Determining Level of Risk – PCRT Assessment*

LEVEL OF RISK
1. *P*RIOR SUICIDAL BEHAVIOR?

> Has the individual tried suicide before? If yes, the risk is higher.
> Is there a history of suicide in the immediate family? If yes, the risk is higher.

Summary

- Previous attempts.
- Family history of suicidal behavior.

2. *C*URRENT SUICIDE PLAN?

> How he/she plans to do it. Does he/she have the means to complete the act?
> Does he/she have a weapon or means to complete the act? The more lethal the method the more likely the death will occur.
> Is he/she prepared to do it? Has he/she actually made specific plans and preparations to complete the act?
> When will it happen? Is there a specific time, or how close to the time is it now?

Summary

- Specific plan. The more specific the plan the higher the risk.

- Access to lethal means. The more lethal the means the higher the risk.

- Has completed preparations. The more complete the preparations, the higher the risk.

- Specific time. The closer the time, the higher the risk.

3. *R* ESOURCES, INTERNAL AND EXTERNAL?

Internal Resources

- High self-esteem and low self-confidence.

- Positive outlook on life.

- Realistic goals and dreams.

- Good physical and mental health.

- Good employment skills.

External Resources

- Many friends.

- Healthy family.

- Stable home.

- Positive role models to follow.

- Access to professional help.

- Satisfying job/academic career.

Summary

- The fewer internal and external resources, the higher the risk.

4. *T* AKE ALL THREATS SERIOUSLY!

- ## *Response to High Assessed Risk*

  - Make a contract with the suicidal person that he/she will not harm him/herself.

  - Do not leave the person alone and don't allow them to leave a safe place. Assign a staff member to maintain visual contact at all times.

  - Contact parents.

  - Inform the student and parents of what has been done.

  - Contact the Mental Health/Social Services/R.C.M.P. immediately.

  - Remove all dangerous articles from the environment.

  - Consider hospitalization or having the individual legally committed to hospital.

  - Have the individual "at risk" develop a survival kit. (See below.)

- ## *Response to Low Assessed Risk*

  > Identify positive traits.

  > Understand negative feelings.

  > Point out that suicide is a permanent solution to a short-term problem.

  > Attempt to help reduce stress.

  > Inform the student and parents of what has been done.

  > Set short-term realistic goals.

  > Build a support network.

  > Negotiate a contract to get further help and that he/she will not harm him/herself.

  > Point out other resources.

  > Strengthen existing coping skills and abilities.

  > Have the individual at risk develop a survival kit.

- ## *Suicide Prevention Survival Kit*

The act of assembling a **survival kit** is a strong message to the potential suicide victim that he/she is willing to stand up to the thoughts of suicide and take active steps toward the preservation of his/her life and future. The individual does not have to wait until all of his/her problems are solved to assemble the kit, do it now and recognize how the simple act of planning for survival can put the individual in touch with his/her own worth and hopefulness. Assembling the survival kit will remind the individual that he/she values his/her life enough to prepare for the difficult times. Contents of the kit should contain items that are important to the individual. Thus contents will vary from one person to another. Things that may be included in the kit are included in the box below.

SURVIVAL KIT
> Pictures of your family or other loved ones, of those for whom it is important to go on living.
> Letters written to you by loved ones.
> A letter written to yourself reminding you of all the things that are valuable and worth living for.
> A few small cherished items.
> A small teapot and a bag of tea to remind you to make yourself a cup of tea before you take any action that may cause harm.
> A chocolate bar or whatever is your favorite treat.

> A tape of your favorite songs. Make it long enough for your self-destructive thoughts to pass.

> Books of poems or mediations that help you gain perspective.

> Objects that support your spiritual perspective (e.g., a Bible with passages marked), or other spiritual resources that can help you through this difficult time.

> A telephone list of those you can trust and to whom you can turn for help and support.

> A list of telephone numbers for the distress line and local hospital.

- ### *Suicide Prevention Contracts*

Another strategy that a helper may take with a person thinking about committing suicide is developing a **contract** with the individual. Contracts may appeal to the troubled individual's sense of fairness and the reliability of his/her word. The contract is a brief document that spells out in clear terms what the individual will do if he/she makes a decision to attempt to commit suicide within a specific period of time. If the person feels the urge to attempt suicide he/she agrees to contact a person or persons identified on the contract. Both the helper and troubled individual sign and date the contract. Contents of a contract may vary depending on the situation and individual(s). Both signatories should have a copy of the signed contract. The troubled individual should be encouraged to keep his/her copy with him/her at all times. A sample contract is included below.

Sample Contract

I,_____, agree that I will not attempt to commit suicide or hurt myself in any way for the next _____ days. If I feel that I will try to break this contract I will contact _____ at _____ immediately if I am at school. If I am not at school I will contact _____ at _____ immediately.

I agree that I will not make any final decision or attempt at committing suicide until I have talked with my counselor/helper directly.

This contract is effective immediately.

_____   _____

Student   Date

_____   _____

Counselor   Date

- ## *Interview Strategy*

According to Ramsay, Tanney, Tierney, & Lang (1994), when interviewing a client who is suicidal it is important to accomplish the following:

> You must first **engage** the individual. Use appropriate attending skills when speaking and listening.

> Next, **identify** whether the individual is thinking about suicide. Ask directly if he/she is thinking about killing him/herself. "Are you thinking about committing suicide?"

> **Inquire** as to the reasons behind the intention of suicide. What is motivating this person to consider suicide?

> Next make your **assessment** (**PCRT**), developed by Ramsay, R., Tanney, B., Tierney, R., & Lang, W. (1994).

> Negotiate a **contract** with the individual. Both team member and the suicidal person must be working toward the same goal.

> Develop a suicide survival kit.

> Last, **follow-through** on whatever you and the individual have agreed upon.

- ## *Things to Remember*

> Most individuals will exhibit warning signs that they are contemplating suicide.

> Talking and asking direct questions about suicide will not increase the risk.

> Suicidal individuals tend to be confused as to whether they really want to die or not.

> If a person attempts suicide and fails he/she may try again. Most don't; however, some do.

> When someone has been depressed but then comes out of the depression, the danger is not over yet.

> Unsuccessful or non-fatal attempts at suicide are not attention getting strategies. They are cries for help.

> Suicide is not a response that has little thought behind it. Most suicide victims have planned the event over a period of time.

> ‣ Individuals should be reminded that suicide is not an alternative for problem solving. It is a permanent solution to short-term difficulties.

> ‣ Suicidal individuals cannot see any alternatives for themselves.

- ### *Uncompleted Suicides*

It is most important for crisis team members to understand the link between **uncompleted suicide** and **completed suicides**. There are four possible motivations that may be associated with non-fatal attempted suicides. They are **attachment**, **escape**, **control**, and **release**. **Attachment** issues may be associated with loss of a partner in a relationship or an attempt to change the existing one. **Escape** may be associated with circumstances in the individual's life that are too difficult to bear e.g. chronic pain, depression, or illness. **Control** may represent an attempt to exert control over someone else. **Release** may be an attempt to eliminate or reduce personal, physical or psychological pressure. Team members should note that the intent of non-fatal suicidal behavior is not necessarily death; it is however, a strong cry for help.

- ### *Post-Suicide*

After a completed suicide has occurred, family, friends and colleagues are concerned with trying to cope with the loss; however, an additional concern is the possibility of more tragedy. Often it has been the view that a suicide recognized by way of a memorial service, tribute, or intervention may encourage copycat suicide attempts. *There is no research to support this view.*

However, it is important to avoid long-term memorializing that may appear to glorify and romanticize the event. Holding a special day, event, or naming something in memory of the deceased is not a recommended practice. This may suggest to others that the choice of suicide was a good one. It is important to encourage thinking that reinforces the idea that other choices and options would have been a more effective way to deal with the problems (Ministry of Education, 1998). Absence of a response by the school will only drive the discussion underground. Parents and staff are advised to help children work through their questions and fears. Students and/or staff who may have come upon the scene or were witnesses to the act may be seriously traumatized. These individuals should be seen apart from the rest of the student body. The event will have a far more serious effect on these individuals. It is most important to identify those students who may be most at risk as a result of a completed suicide. A list of possible things to consider when developing this list of students follows:

> Individuals who were especially close the deceased.

> Siblings or relatives.

> Close friends and those who felt they were confidants to the deceased.

> Individuals who express extreme signs of grief and guilt over the incident.

> Individuals who have attempted suicide in the past.

> Individuals with significant personal problems and who feel there are no resolution to their problems.

> Individuals who have recently lost a significant member of their family.

> Individuals who feel responsible for the death, e.g. "I should have known, or "I should have done something, it's my fault."

> Remember to record the date of the event. This anniversary date will have significance next year when many students remember the initial incident.

VIOLENT CRISES

Violence and conflict affect the educational process and reduce its effectiveness. Students who either experience violence directly or indirectly have increased anxiety and fear that will have an effect upon their academic performance and commitment to education. An overall safety plan for crisis intervention requires a thoughtful process for identifying security needs, developing intervention and prevention techniques, evaluating physical facilities, and providing communication between students and staff. Note that sexual assault is a crime of violence and is included here.

- ### *Response To Violent Crisis*

When a violent crisis does occur it is of utmost importance to have an effective crisis intervention plan. The immediate after affect of a violent crisis produces three waves of reaction that can overwhelm staff and existing resources.

1. Police and rescue workers will arrive. Police will make decisions regarding student and staff safety, disarm the situation, and start their investigation.

2. The media will arrive. The media will not give up because of the high impact of violence; they will do their best to get the story. Follow the **Guidelines for Handling the Media**. When responding to media questions, the following information may be helpful.

   - No one is hurt.

   - The police have the situation under control.

   - Please do not attempt to come to the school. Police are not allowing people in the school at this time.

   - The school will notify you when and where you can pick your child up.

   - The media will keep you informed as to when and where you can pick your child up.

3. Anxious parents will either begin to arrive at the school or flood the school with telephone calls. Be prepared to answer calls.

- ### *Guidelines for Police Intervention*

It should be noted that before requesting direct police intervention, every effort to settle a disruption should be made by school staff; however the police department should be notified of the school disturbance as a matter of record and reference for any future need for assistance. School and police officials respond to disturbance in accordance to the level of intensity. The three levels of intensity are:

Level 1

The disturbance is confined to one area and without threat to students or staff. School personnel respond by containing or removing persons involved with minimum interruption.

No direct police intervention.

Level 2

The disturbance is mobile and/or poses a direct threat to students and staff. The school remains open, but police officers isolate the disruptive activity, detain individuals

involved, and terminate the threat of escalation. As many school personnel as possible
should carry out routine school operations during the disturbance.
Direct police intervention.

Level 3

The disturbance prevents regular school operations from continuing, there are serious
threats to students and staff safety, and the situation is no longer within the school's
control. The principal requests police assistance in accordance with guidelines previously
established in a written memorandum of understanding between police officials and the
Principal and/or School Division/District. Police officers at the scene close the school
and assume responsibility for controlling the situation. Authority to end the disruption
shifts from the Principal and/or area superintendent to the police officer in charge.
Responsibility for maintaining safety and order among students and staff, and
responsibility for the facility remain with the school's Principal and area superintendent.
Direct police intervention.

- ***Situational Assessment***

When a critical incident develops due to an act of violence and prior to police
intervention, the Principal should conduct a **situational assessment**. Questions to ask
when conducting the assessment should include:

> Are rival gangs or groups at school involved?

> Is discipline or crowd control going to be a problem?

> Who witnessed the incident?

> Are the witnesses likely to be traumatized?

> Which groups are likely to be affected?

> Are there any particular historical, social, personal, or cultural factors that may
> affect the situation?

> Is the school safe and secure for the students?

> Is there a need to call in police officers?

> Which classes are likely to be affected the most?

> Are there staff members who may be affected more than others?

> Are there any legal issues that could affect the crisis response team or school?

- ### *Preparing for Police Involvement*

It is important to have specific procedures established involving the police responding to violence or a violent crisis at the school. These procedures should be developed in cooperation with the appropriate police officials, school Principal, and area Superintendent.

1. Generally, the Principal declares an emergency and is responsible for requesting assistance through direct communication with the area superintendent. A predetermined **"Emergency Operations Center"** (EOC) is established where the Principal or area superintendent works with emergency services and clearly defines the responsibility of each person.

2. Establish emergency procedures that include notifying local law enforcement agencies, the fire department, and medical assistance agencies as appropriate. In some counties, law enforcement officials handle contacts with other agencies in the event of an emergency.

3. Post and regularly update a checklist of equipment and emergency telephone numbers. This should be posted in the staff room.

- ### *Effective Communication*

Another important component of any crisis plan is a procedure that enables effective communication with all school staff and external agencies that may be assisting in the management of a critical incident.

> Establish a clear communication system that signals an emergency, and when the crisis has passed, signal an "all clear." The signal should be distinguishable from those that designate class periods, and should be established prior to an emergency situation.

> Establish a rumor control/information post in a location accessible to parents, interested community members, and media, to handle inquiries in an orderly

fashion. This post would provide a system for swift parental contact and an outside line for specific communication to community transportation volunteers.

> The Principal should act as the police contact person for the school.

> Designate a spokesperson to advise the media and respond to questions and concerns.

> Develop a procedure for establishing and maintaining control of the media and onlookers who could impede operations. Have the School District/Division's communication officer provide updated information on the status of a crisis at regular intervals so as to minimize rumors and interruptions.

> Develop procedures for keeping family members and other relatives informed about students enrolled in the school.

> Select a person for taking messages and recording incidents for documentation purposes.

> Establish a system for message delivery and backup should initial communications breakdown.

> After the crisis has subsided and students have been dismissed, debrief all staff members about the emergency and the procedures taken.

- ### *General Safety Considerations*

During any violent critical incident it is critical that all staff and students are safe from further trauma and other sources of potential danger.

> Devise a signal for announcing an emergency situation. This signal may differ depending on the type of emergency and available devices.

> Identify who can declare an emergency and under what conditions. The principal should make this decision.

> Develop a procedure for identifying safe and injured students.

> Identify an adequate location and a procedure for administering first aid.

> Develop a systematic process for releasing students to parents or guardians that includes a **sign-out** procedure and verification of persons authorized to pick up students. Provide a description of the process in other languages for non-English speaking parents.

- Establish a "clean up" committee to be called in immediately following a disaster to completely clean and to repair damages so that the school can open as soon as the following day. Identify possible professional non-school personnel to do the clean up, especially in the event of gunshot victims.

- Identify a crisis intervention team of psychologists and counselors to be called to provide debriefing and counseling for any resulting trauma affecting students and staff members.

- Establish an orderly dismissal procedure; e.g., dismissal by floors or sections, in a manner that everyone understands.

- Provide parents with information in their first language, if possible, regarding relevant elements of the emergency plan, so they are prepared and know what to expect.

- Conduct periodic practice drills to ensure procedures for dismissal run smoothly.

- Establish a "buddy system" for all students, especially significantly disabled students.

- ### *Personal Safety and Security*

During any violent crisis intervention, the safety of crisis response team members are a serious concern. To ensure that every attempt is made to maintain personal safety, the following procedures are suggested when conducting counseling, defusing, or debriefing sessions with violent students while in counselor's office, classroom, or other office:

- Interview with a partner, if possible.

- Remove any potential weapons e.g. heavy ashtray, letter opener, paperweight etc.

- Seat individual next to the door.

- When greeting individuals notice anything strange about their words, behavior, or dress.

- Conduct a visual frisk.

- Note the individual's body language.

- Do not remain after school hours with a violent student unless you have a partner.

- Inform individual that you have a partner in the outer office.

- Get in the habit of asking yourself "what if" this happens.

> ⊳ Be prepared for unexpected behavior.

> ⊳ Sit with your feet flat on the floor with your hands unfolded in your lap; lean slightly forward. This conveys interest and concern and it allows you to respond immediately if threatened physically.

> ⊳ Attempt to speak with the individual at eye level.

> ⊳ Avoid standing over the individual. If he/she chooses to remain standing do the same.

> ⊳ If standing have your feet about shoulder width apart, one foot slightly behind the other, and weight on the rear leg, knees slightly bent, hands folded but not interlocked.

> ⊳ Avoid sitting in a corner. There is no escape there.

> ⊳ Do not turn your back on a violent individual or allow them to walk behind you.

> ⊳ Know where your nearest emergency telephone is located.

SUDDEN LOSS

As a crisis team member you may be called to respond to a traumatic event that involves both a permanent loss of an individual by death and the temporary loss of an individual from the community due to incarceration. For example a motor vehicle accident occurs and one individual is killed whereas the other individual is not, but has contributed to the death of the first person by way of impaired driving or other form of negligence. You have to deal with the feelings and emotions surrounding the precipitating event (critical incident) associated with the loss and grief over the death, as well as the loss of the individual who will be removed from the community and incarcerated due his/her actions. These situations often create conflicting feelings and tend to polarize groups of students and community members. Response should first focus on dealing with the critical incident and conducting the debriefing. The debriefings should follow the outlines presented earlier in this manual. Individuals closest to both victims should be debriefed individually.

It is important to note that regression is a common response to loss. The more serious and sudden the loss, the more the individuals' cycle of distress, coping abilities, and withdrawal resemble **acute traumatic stress**. Another response to sudden loss may be **acute grief response**. Individuals experiencing acute grief response are completely incapacitated. Conducting individual and classroom debriefings will be helpful. It is important to assess individual functioning, safety needs, and available support.

A TERMINALLY ILL CHILD

It is possible that you may have a student in your class who is terminally ill. Often questions arise about the individual because he or she may have undergone obvious physical changes, missed a significant amount of time from school, or been too weak to participate in various school activities. Classmates may start to ask difficult questions about the child. The teacher may not know how to answer the students' questions about the child. First of all, keep in mind that it is important for the sick child to be in school. Children who are terminally ill still want to learn, play, and be with friends. Second, parents tend to hang on to hope so tightly that the school may be unable to prepare classmates for the eventual death of their peer. The question is how do you prepare classmates? Medical information is confidential and can not be discussed in class or elsewhere unless the parent or parents have given written permission. Efforts should be made to obtain parent permission to discuss the subjects with classmates; however, if permission is not granted there are a few things the classroom teacher can do to help prepare the other students. Listed below are some suggestions presented by Petersen & Straub (1992):

> First of all ensure that the sick child is not in the classroom at the time of the discussion. This would only create more stress and anxiety for that person. Also, having the sick child present will tend to hamper the discussion.

> Try to determine what other classmates have noticed about the child that sets him or her apart from the others.

> Gradually introduce the fact that this person is seriously ill.

> Solicit views from other students about the illness. This gives the teacher a reference as to how classmates understand and interpret their peer's behavior and condition.

> Inform the class about this person's illness. It is important that other students understand that they can not catch this illness. You will likely have to repeat a number of times that others can not catch the illness.

> Next tell the others what will happen to their classmate.

> At this point it important to tell the students what they can do to help make things happier for their classmate.

> Remember that elementary students will have to be reminded more often than junior and senior high school students.

> Keep in mind that children are often aware that one of their peers may be quite different from them. This may not be a source of concern for them. In other words, "if it isn't broken, don't try to fix it."

FAMILY CRISIS

In most provinces and territories it is not the responsibility of school based crisis teams to respond to family crises. However, it is helpful and indeed important for helpers to have an understanding of the home situation of students who are exhibiting signs and symptoms of either **acute traumatic stress** or **acute grief response.** All students need a strong support system at home. Students coming from families experiencing some form of crisis likely do not have much in the way of support at home. According to Steel & Raider (1991), families experiencing some form of crisis may exhibit the following signs:

> Emotionally cool, detached, and aloof;

> Emotionally explosive and unpredictable;

> Unwilling to communicate;

> Unwilling to ask for help or accept it;

> Closed to different ways of coping;

> Absence of family in decision making;

> Denial, withdrawal, or avoidance of inherent conflicts within a crisis;

> ⊳ Loss of parental direction, guidance, and support;

> ⊳ Substance abuse; and/or,

> ⊳ Scape-goating and blaming.

LARGE SCALE DISASTER

Large scale or natural disasters affect the entire community. Such disasters include earthquakes, floods, fires, hurricanes, tsunamis, or tornadoes etc. The effects of a natural disaster are community wide and cause tremendous destruction. The damage is sudden and irreversible. People feel isolated. Recovery from natural disasters tends to be more difficult than recovering from critical incidents involving the death of an individual. Recovery is inhibited by the nature of the wide spread destruction and the lack of personal control experienced by individuals. Other factors that affect recovery include the loss of personal possessions, inadequate financial resources, and possible inaccurate reporting by the press. Also, during a natural disaster there may be looting and loss of communication with other areas.

School-aged children who experience natural or large-scale disasters experience similar reactions as those during other crises. The predominant reaction by elementary school children tends to be fear. Fear is exhibited by a general sense of anxiety, hyperactivity, and flashbacks; there may an increase in the number of stomach illnesses and headaches. As a result of a large scale disaster adolescents tend to miss more school and there may also be an increase in substance abuse. It is important to note that these emotions are easily rekindled by associative factors that remind the victims of the original disaster.

MARINE DISASTER

Marine disasters that involve numerous passengers or large ships are no accident. Almost invariably they are the consequence of a chain of events. The removal of any one link will prevent the disaster occurring or at least mitigate the outcome. A well prepared, effective disaster plan will be the very last link in that chain and the only chance to ensure that a bad situation does not get worse simply because of a lack of planning. Marine disasters can be especially difficult and dangerous due to water conditions such as temperature, wave height, location, and the presence of other potentially dangerous materials on the vessel. Marine disasters involve a number of different responders. The military has traditionally conducted search and rescue operations. In the event that an aircraft has gone down at sea the civil aviation authority will be involved. If there is concern about dangerous pollutants leaking into the sea specialized teams or agencies trained to conduct such clean up and recovery will be involved. Furthermore rescue of large numbers of people at sea or in open water is slow unless other ships are close by.

Marine disasters may also involve discharge of oil or other dangerous pollutants into the environment. Consequently numerous other agencies and governments may be involved in any rescue operation. Coordination and cooperation between governments and organizations is imperative in order to launch a successful rescue operation.

THREAT ASSESSMENT

Due to the increase in terrorism and violence in schools, Departments of Education and School Administrations have been encouraged develop Multidisciplinary Teams to conduct **Threat Assessments** and **Risk Assessments**. **Threat Assessment** is the process of collecting data through structured interviews to determine the level of risk that may be posed by a threat maker against a target or multiple targets and plan an appropriate strategy to reduce the potential risk to the target or targets. There are four types of threats; **Direct Threats**, **Indirect Threats**, **Veiled Threats**, and **Conditional Threats**.

Direct Threats
These threats are verbalized, written, or gestured and indicate direct action to be taken against one or more individuals or an object.

Indirect Threats

These threats are verbalized or written and suggest that an action will be taken against one or more individuals or objects. The difference between direct and indirect is that the threat is not clearly indicated but is implied.

Veiled Threats

These threats are not as clear in terms of language. The threat can be cloaked with ambiguity in terms of the intended action. These threats may be uttered against one or more individuals or an object.

Conditional Threats

These threats are uttered as an ultimatum if some other intended action or condition is not met to the satisfaction of the threat maker.

Although the belief that the best predictor of future behavior is past behavior there are a few problems with this view. *First*, many people engage in violent behavior but never come close to becoming murderers. *Second*, many individuals who have turned guns and knives on others had no history of violence prior to the act of becoming murders. These individuals have been called "**Empty Vessels**" due to the lack of connection many had to healthy mature adults as well as their lack of clear identity, place, or purpose.

Risk Assessment is the process of determining if an individual previously identified through the **Threat Assessment** process poses a risk to a target or targets identified by the individual under investigation. In most cases the individual has not actually threatened to kill a target or targets but that individual's behavior or ideation has been increasing in violence that suggest that their potential for violence may be escalating.

- ### *Responsibility*

According to Cameron, J.K., (2004), any person in a school having knowledge of high-risk behavior or having reasonable grounds to believe there is a potential for high-risk behavior shall promptly report the information to the school principal. No action will be taken against a person who makes a report unless the report is made maliciously and without reasonable grounds. In such cases, the person making the malicious report shall be dealt with according to Department of Education or District policy, where applicable.

- *__Level of Action__*

There are four levels of response that may result from the information gathered by the Multidisciplinary Threat Assessment Team. The level of response implemented by an Administrator is in reaction to the perceived or anticipated level of risk indicated by a threat maker. These four levels can be categorized as **Immediate Risk Situations**, **Threat Making Behaviors**, **Worrisome Behaviors**, and **Exceptional Cases**.

1. **Immediate Risk Situations** are those situations that include armed intruders inside the building or on the periphery who may pose an immediate risk to a target or targets. The school Principal should immediately contact the police and take the necessary steps to ensure the safety of all students and staff.

2. **Threat Making Behaviors** are those students age twelve years or older who are believed to have contravened Section 264.1 (1) of the Criminal Code of Canada which states that an individual "who in any manner, knowingly utters, conveys or causes any person to receive a threat…to cause death or bodily harm" has committed an offence. In these instances as well, the school Principal should immediately contact the police and take the necessary steps to ensure the safety of all students and staff.

3. **Worrisome Behaviors** are those behaviors or a threat maker that cause concern for members of a School Administration or Divisional/District Office personnel that indicates or suggests that the threat maker's behavior is, or may be, perceived to be moving toward a greater risk of violent behavior. The majority of threat related behaviors from kindergarten to grade twelve fall into this category. When students utter generalized threats the Principal shall contact the School Psychologist or Counselor for consultation to determine if information or incident warrants further action.

4. **High Profile Worrisome Behaviors** occur in a setting where there is an audience that may be traumatized and their reactions to the incident may trigger

a broader trauma response within the school or community. These situations may arise due to elevated sensitivity by some students, staff, or parents in the aftermath of high profile traumatic events such as school shootings or other violent incidents.

- ### *Threat Assessment Report*

Following a Threat Assessment a **Threat Assessment Report** should be written. This report is usually written by the Principal in collaboration with team members. Its contents should include the following which is adapted from the "Guide for Preventing and Responding to School Violence," published by the International Association of Chiefs of Police:

> ▷ Name of the threat maker and his/her relationship to the school and recipient;
>
> ▷ Names of the target or potential targets;
>
> ▷ When and where the incident occurred;
>
> ▷ What happened immediately prior to the incident;
>
> ▷ The specific language of the threat;
>
> ▷ Physical conduct that would support intent to follow through on a threat;
>
> ▷ How the threat maker appeared emotionally and physically;
>
> ▷ Names of others who were directly involved and any actions they took;
>
> ▷ How the incident ended;
>
> ▷ Names of any witnesses;
>
> ▷ What happened to the threat maker after the incident;
>
> ▷ What happened to other individuals directly involved after the incident;
>
> ▷ Names of any administrators, teachers, or staff and how they responded;
>
> ▷ Any history leading up to the event;
>
> ▷ The steps that have been taken to ensure the threat will not be carried out; and,
>
> ▷ Suggestions for preventing school violence in the future.

PART 10. DEVELOPING A COMPREHENSIVE CRISIS PLAN

SUMMARY OF PROCEDURES

Listed below is a summary of specific strategies and procedures that have been detailed in this manual. As previously described, they are implemented at various times during a critical incident.

Defusing Emotions

Conducting defusing sessions is one of the first attempts to help individuals start to face the critical incident. Anger, hostility, and extreme emotionality may characterize the sessions. The procedure used in defusing emotions is unstructured and usually occurs during the first day of an incident. Counselors and crisis team members most often conduct these sessions. Teachers familiar with the process may conduct defusing sessions as well. Defusing sessions are usually limited to approximately eight to ten individuals.

Group Debriefing

The procedure used in the group discussion usually occurs after things have started to calm down (during the second day). Group debriefings follow a semi-structured format and may be facilitated by the counselor, crisis team member, or teacher familiar with the procedure. Group debriefings represent the first step in helping individuals put the incident and their reactions in perspective. Debriefing groups should be limited to approximately fourteen individuals. Although anger and denial may characterize some of the groups, there may be some signs of acceptance.

Solution Focused Counseling

The solution-focused approach to counseling is mentioned here because it tends to be quite effective. Its success may be attributed, in part, to the fact that the solutions are student generated and focus on what the individual is doing correctly. Counselors or crisis team members usually implement this process. Sessions are conducted on an individual basis and may be utilized throughout and for some, after a critical incident. A full range of emotions may characterize individual sessions.

Individual Debriefing

The individual debriefing procedure follows a semi-structured format. Individual debriefings are usually implemented during the first two days of a critical incident. As a more formal attempt to help the individuals deal with the critical incident. This is the most appropriate way to debrief those individuals who were closest to the victim, felt they were responsible for the death, or could have prevented it. A full range of emotions may characterize these sessions.

Classroom Debriefing

Classroom debriefings provide an opportunity to present the facts as they are known and clarify any misinformation to a larger group. The format is structured and conducted by the counselor, crisis team member, or teacher familiar with the procedure. Debriefings are usually started on the first day of a critical incident and follow into the second day. Classroom debriefings vary in length, but usually do not last longer than thirty to forty-five minutes. Reactions during a debriefing tend to be much more subdued when compared with individual sessions.

Healing Circle

First Nations use this procedure when dealing with a critical incident. The format tends to be unstructured. Healing circles are used to help individuals deal with the incident and understand their feelings. Use of a familiar object to identify the person speaking is important. This procedure usually occurs during the first two days. Healing circles may be implemented in a classroom. These sessions are conducted by a First Nations elder, counselor, crisis team member, or teachers familiar with the procedure. Healing circles may last between forty-five minutes to one and one-half hours.

Student Drop-In Center

This strategy is used when a critical incident affects a junior/senior high school. The Center is often set up in the school library as this tends to be a quiet place and is staffed by either two counselors or teaching staff. The drop-in center is set up the first day. The Drop In Center is a quiet place where students can go when they may wish to be alone or are having difficulty coping in the classroom. All teachers and staff should be told that students may go to the center at any time. Permission is not needed, but they should notify the teacher where they are going. Defusing sessions and group discussions may take place in the drop-in center.

Crisis Center

It is most helpful if a specific room can be set up as the Crisis Center. This is where all the work, strategy sessions, and planning during the critical incident will take place. The room should be equipped with a chalk or white board, large table, chairs, coffee machine, and a dedicated crisis telephone line. The room should be private and not normally accessed by staff or visitors to the school so the traditional staff room is not a good location for the Crisis Center. Staff debriefings may be done here so keep lots of tissue on hand for use during these debriefings.

Media Center

If a critical incident develops into a lengthy one it is helpful to set up a separate room as a Media_Center. The Center should be equipped with telephones, computer, fax, photocopier coffee/tea dispenser, and a white or chalkboard. This is where scheduled meetings with the media may be held.

Hall Monitors

Specific staff persons are assigned to patrol the halls and washrooms to ensure that students are not gathering in large groups. This is an attempt to keep students who are less affected by the incident from becoming significantly influenced by the emotionality of those closest to the victim. This tends to be more necessary at the junior and senior grade level as adolescents tend to feed off the emotional reactions of those in an emotionally fragile state. Hall monitors are used during the first two or three days of the incident. Monitors can watch for any signs of shrines or other such symbols being made of the victim's desk or locker. This is especially important if a critical incident is due to suicide.

Information Letter

This is a letter prepared and sent out by the Principal. It is prepared the first day and sent home with every student at school. It contains specific information to help parents assist their child in dealing with the incident. The letter should also state what resources are available to students, the steps being taken at the school, an acknowledgement of the loss, and ways in which parents can help their children cope with the incident. Also provided on the back of the letter is a list of community resources.

Staff Debriefing

Staff debriefing is the same as classroom debriefing and it should be conducted within the first two or three days of the incident. The format is semi-structured and may be conducted by the counselor, crisis team member, school psychologist, or an external resource person although it is preferable to have an external resource person conduct the debriefing because a critical incident affects all school staff. Attendance at the debriefing should be strongly encouraged. All teaching and support staff (secretarial, custodial, et al) should attend. This session may last from one to two hours.

Operational Debriefing

The operational debriefing, similar to the classroom debriefing, follows a structured format to debrief school based and District/Division crisis response teams. The debriefings should be conducted at their respective locations. School based and District/Division teams should not be debriefed together. The Principal or counselor may conduct the debriefing at the school, or an external resource person may be asked to conduct it. Likewise, the District/Division crisis team leader or external resource person should conduct the District/Division debriefing. The debriefing should occur within two weeks after the incident has passed. These teams are concerned with improving their performance.

Single Entry/Exit

Establishing one location to enter and exit the school enables school staff to prevent seriously distraught students from leaving the building unescorted or without parental permission. A single entry and exit also enables staff to better determine who is in the building.

SUMMARY OF FORMS

A short description and rationale for each form in the manual and workbook is provided below. Each form can be modified to meet your needs. If you wish an electronic copy of these forms, please contact either of the contributors by e-mail. Electronic versions would allow modifications of the forms to specific settings and also would allow, with modifications, school officials to complete them on line when appropriate. The original purchaser of this manual is given permission to copy forms for crisis intervention purposes.

Note: The checklists, logs, records, and forms in this manual are included as a guide only. It is the responsibility of the Principal, in collaboration with the school-based crisis team, to determine which will be used.

Rapid Response Checklists

These are located in Appendix 3. They have been divided in to three groups: Immediate Response, Specific Crises, Specific Assessments, Specific Interventions, and Recording/Monitoring. They can be used when you want to ensure those specific steps and actions have taken place.

School/Community Crisis Response Team

Complete this to provide a list of the current school based team members and their chief responsibility. Space is provided for alternate members.

Telephone Contact Tree

This form provides a quick and systematic manner for contacting all staff should a critical incident occur after hours.

Crisis Information Form

This form should be completed and sent off to the area Superintendent. It contains all the essential factual information about the current critical incident.

Initial Crisis Management Plan

Completion of this form provides a detailed record of the known facts about the critical incident, role responsibilities, activities for children, response to media, considerations about the memorial and more. This form should be retained at the school as it is intended to assist the Principal when developing a response plan to a critical incident and to serve as a permanent record in case of any discrepancy. It may serve as the school critical incident plan or used as additional or preliminary information when developing a plan for the school.

Day-One Operational Checklist

This checklist contains most of the important actions and considerations that should take place the first day when responding to a critical incident. It is in checklist format and every item is either checked off yes or no. This makes it quick to complete and easy to scan to determine which actions have or have not been taken. Most school crisis intervention plans tend to be different from each other. Some items on this checklist may not be included in your school crisis plan or some may not be checked off because it has been determined that the action is not necessary for the current situation. Item selection for your school plan will depend upon the nature of the critical incident, the available resources, and individual approach to responding to crises.

Day-Two Operational Checklist

This checklist contains most of the important actions and considerations that should continue into the second day of a critical incident. Some items on this checklist may not be included in your school crisis plan and some items may not be included because it has been determined that the action is not necessary for the current situation. Item selection for your school plan will depend upon the nature of the critical incident, the available resources, and individual approach to responding to crises.

Day-Three Operational Checklist

This checklist contains most of the important actions and considerations that should continue into the third day of a critical incident. Focus of some items is towards restoring routine and structure. Some items on this checklist may not be included in your school crisis plan or some may not be checked off because it has been determined that the action is not necessary for the current situation. Item selection for your school plan will depend upon the nature of the critical incident, the available resources, and individual approach to responding to crises.

Telephone Log

Complete this to retain a record of all incoming or outgoing calls about the critical incident. You can determine at a glance if a follow-up is required.

Critical Incident Alert Form

This form is completed and sent to all school staff. It provides known factual information about the critical incident. This will ensure that all school staff have been informed about the facts of the incident.

Classroom Support Request Log

Complete this log to determine which teachers have requested additional support in their classrooms during a critical incident and the support persons assigned to them.

Student Sign Out Log

This is used to record the names of students coming into and leaving the school during a critical incident. You can record whether parents have been contacted to pick up a student, or if the student has left unescorted.

School Visitors Log

This form can be used to monitor and record the names of individuals visiting the school during a critical incident.

Critical Incident Intervention Request

The Principal may complete this form when specifically requesting crisis intervention assistance from the District/Department of Education. It is a good idea to complete this form if there are any questions regarding possible litigation. When this form is completed it provides a detailed record of the request.

External Support Request Record

This provides a record of all additional sources of support that have been contacted by the Principal to provide assistance to the school-based crisis team. You can quickly determine which sources have been contacted and whether the support has been provided.

Referral For Counseling

Complete this form to record the names of all students referred for counseling during a critical incident. You can note whether parents have been contacted. Names followed by an (*) indicate that they are considered to be "high risk" individuals.

Suicide Prevention Contract

If you are dealing with an individual who has been identified as "at risk" for attempting suicide you may wish to negotiate a contract with him/her whereby he/she agrees to abide by the conditions set out in the contract.

Classroom Announcement Form

This is completed by the Principal and given to every classroom teacher. It contains essential factual information about a critical incident that a teacher should present to students in his/her classroom. A brief description of teacher responsibilities is included.

Media Information Release

This form is used to provide specific information to the media about a critical incident and the response taken at the school level. District/Department crisis members may also complete this form. Specific restrictions are stated to the media and their cooperation is requested. For reasons of confidentiality, remember not to state the victim(s) names unless approved by the parent(s)/guardian(s).

Memorial Service Record

Complete this form to record all the necessary information about a school based memorial service.

Critical Incident Response Summary

Complete this form to provide a summary of the steps taken when responding to a critical incident. Entries do not have to be in-depth, but should provide documented evidence that a particular intervention or action took place. Completion of this form could be useful if there are concerns about possible litigation. As well, having the steps documented will help in developing and refining your school crisis intervention plan.

School Critical Incident Plan Review

Complete this form on an annual or semiannual basis. Use of this form will maintain a degree of quality assurance for your school crisis intervention plan.

Follow-Up Checklist

Complete this form to ensure that all specified follow-up activities and responsibilities have been completed.

Critical Incident Report

This form provides a concise summary of the critical incident and the response taken by the School Based Crisis Team or District/Department Crisis Team. Completion of this form could be helpful if litigation results from the critical incident.

Critical Incident Log

The School-Based Crisis Team and/or District/Department Crisis Team use this form to track and record all critical incidents that have been responded to.

CONCLUSION

Rather than passively hoping that a crisis will not occur and that trauma will not result, it is far better to take a proactive position and develop a school crisis intervention plan. Unfortunately, the response to and management of a crisis often occurs during the event. Prior to any crisis event, school officials in positions of authority should develop a plan with their staff and in conjunction with local health, social services and law enforcement agencies. Intervention plans covering a wide range of traumatic contingencies should be rehearsed. It appears only logical for schools to assume a proactive posture in their communities by developing a crisis response plan and thus minimizing the potential negative behavioral, social/emotional and academic effects on students.

This manual is intended to serve as a guide for responding to school-based critical incidents. The material contained in this manual cannot supersede appropriate training and experience in responding to various critical incidents. The involvement of Divisional/District personnel (school psychologists, counselors, and/or nurses) who are trained to respond in crisis situations should always be considered as a support to school staff.

Numerous forms and checklists have been specifically developed to help team members record and track actions and procedures implemented during a critical incident. It is through the use of these forms and checklists, as well as implementing some or all of the procedures contained in this manual, that a school crisis plan will start to emerge. Other factors that will influence development of the crisis plan include the availability and willingness of staff to serve as team members and access to relevant in-service education.

BIBLIOGRAPHY

Alberta Education Response Center (1992). Bereavement and Loss Manual: For Administrators and Teachers. Edmonton, Alberta.

American Psychiatric Association (1995). Diagnostic and Statistical Manual of Mental Disorders-Fourth Edition.

Blurton, J. (January, 2005). Dealing with Children and Catastrophic Events. www.talhk.com.

Cameron, J.K. (2004). Assessing Violence Potential: Protocol for Dealing with High-Risk Student Behaviors, Fourth Edition.

Cameron, J.K., Sawyer, D., Urbanoski, R.N. (2004). Strategic Interviewing in Threat Assessment Level II.

Clayton, J. Crisis Intervention Guide. Halifax Regional School Board, Nova Scotia.

Coquitlam School District (1996). Coping with Sudden Death in the School Setting.

Delta School District (1997). School Critical Incident Response Protocol.

Educational Service (1997). Quick Response: A Step-by-Step Guide to Crisis Management. District 105, Yakima, Washington

Everstine, D. S, & Everstine, L. (1993). People in Crisis. New York: Brunner and Mazel Inc.

Fairchild, T.N. (1986). Crisis Intervention Strategies for School-Based Helpers. Illinois: Charles C. Thomas Publishers.

Greenstone, J. L., & Leviton, S.C. (1993). Elements of Crisis Intervention. California: Pacific Grove.

Johnson, K., (1993). School Crisis Management. California: Hunter House.

Johnson, K., (1989). Trauma in the Lives of Children. California: Hunter House.

Johnson, K., (1987). Classroom Crisis. California: Hunter House.

Mitchell, J., & Everly, G.S. (1993). Critical Incident Stress Debriefing: An Operations Manual for the Prevention of Traumatic Stress Among Emergency Service and Disaster Workers. Ellicott City: Chevron Publications.

Petersen, S., & Straub, R. L., (1992). School Crisis Survival Guide. New York: The Center for Applied Research in Education.

Qualicum School District (1997). Sudden Death/Suicide Protocols.

Ramsay, R., Tanney, B., Tierney, R., & Lang, W., (1994). <u>Suicide Intervention Handbook</u>. Calgary: Living Works Education Inc.

Rando, T. <u>Grieving: How to go on Living When Someone You Love Dies</u>.

Roberts, A., (1990). <u>Crisis Intervention Handbook: Assessment, Treatment and Research</u>. California: Wadsworth Publishing Company.

Steele, W., & Raider, M. (1991). <u>Working with Families in Crisis</u>. New York: The Guilford Press.

White, P.F. & Peat, D.W. (2005). <u>Critical Incident Manual.</u> Care Society, Republic of Maldives.

APPENDIX 1

SUGGESTED READINGS

Aguilera, D.C. (1994). Crisis Intervention: Theory and Methodology seventh edition. St. Louis: Mosby.

Alexander, C.A. (1993). Stress among police body handlers. A long-term follow-up. British Journal of Psychiatry, 163, 806-808.

Armstrong, K., O'Callahan, W., & Marmer, C.R. (1991). Debriefing Red Cross disaster personnel: the multiple stressor debriefing model. Journal of Traumatic Stress, 4, 581-593.

Berah, E., Jones, H.J., & Valent, P. (1982). The experience of a mental health team involved in the early phase of a disaster. Australian and New Zealand Journal of Psychiatry, 18, 354-358.

Bisson, J.I. & Deahl, M. (1994). Psychological debriefing and prevention of post-traumatic stress. British Journal of Psychiatry, 165, 717-720.

Burns, C., & Harm, N.J. (1993). Emergency nurses' perception of critical incidents and stress debriefing. Journal of Emergency Nursing, 19, (5), 431436. ·

Blurton, J. (January, 2005). Dealing with Children and Catastrophic Events. www.talhk.com.

Corneil, W. (1993). Prevalence of post-traumatic stress disorders in a metropolitan fire department. Dissertation submitted to the school of Hygiene and Public Health, the Johns Hopkins University, Baltimore, Maryland.

Dunning, C. (1988). Intervention strategies for emergency workers. In M. Lystad (ed.), Mental Health Response to Mass Emergencies: Theory and Practice. (p.p. 284-304). New York: Brunner/Mazel.

Dyregrov, A. (1989). Caring for helpers in disaster situations: psychological debriefings. Disaster management, 2, 25-30.

Everstine, D.S., & Everstine, L. (1993). The Trauma Response. New York: W.W. Norton.

Green, B.L. (1990). Defining Trauma: Terminology and genetic stressor dimensions. Journal of Applied Social Psychology, 20, 1632-1642.

Griffith, J.A. & Watts, R. (1992). The Kempsey and Grafton Buss Crashes: The Aftermath. East Lismore: Instructional Design Solutions.

Hoff, L.A., People in Crisis third edition. Redwood City: Addison-Wesley.

Horowitz, M. (1976). The Stress Response Syndrome. New York: Jackson Aronson.

Kenardy, J.A., Webster, R.A., Lewin, T.J., & Carr, D.L. (1996). Stress debriefing patterns of recovery following a natural disaster. Journal of Traumatic Stress, 9, 37-49.

Lane, P.S. (1994). Critical incident stress debriefing for health care workers. Omega, 28, (4), 301-315.

McCammon, S., Durham, T.W., Allison, E.J., & Williamson, J.E. (1988). Emergency workers' cognitive appraisal and coping with traumatic events. The Journal of Traumatic Stress, 1, 353-372.

McConkey, N. (1999). Solving school problems: A solution-focused approach. In press.

Mitchell, J., & Bray, G. (1990). Emergency Service Stress. Englewood Cliffs, N.J.: Prentice-Hall.

Mitchell, J. (1983). When disaster strikes: The critical incident stress debriefing process. Journal of Emergency Medical Services, 8, 36-39.

Mitchell, J. (1986). Living dangerously: why some firefighters take risks on the job. Firehouse, 11, (8), 50-51, 63.

Mitchell, J., & Everly, G.S. (1997). The Scientific Evidence for the critical incident stress management. Journal of Emergency Medical Services, 22, (January) 86-93.

Ostrow, L.S. (1996). Critical Incident Stress Management: Is it worth it? Journal of Emergency Medical Services, 21, (August) 29-36.

Raphael, B. (1986). When Disaster Strikes. New York: Basic Books.

Raphael, B., Meldrum, L., & McFarlane, A.C. (1995). Does debriefing after psychological trauma work? British Medical Journal, 310, 1479-1480.

Raphael, B., Singh, B. & Bradbbury, L. (1980). Disaster: The helper's perspective. Medical Journal of Australia, 2, 445-447.

APPENDIX 2

Pocket Reference Cards

DEFUSING EMOTIONS

1. GROUND RULES
- Confidentiality, what is said in here stays in here.
- No put-downs.
- No interruptions.
- Speak only for yourself.

2. FORMAT
- Discuss facts and feelings.
- What did you see?
- What have you heard about the incident?
- What did you feel?

3. IDENTIFY NEEDS
- Sort out past and present events.

4. REACTIONS
- Watch for range of individual reactions to the incident.
- Note general amusement, numbness, unaffected.

5. WHEN IT'S OVER
- Keep discussion gently focused until it goes its normal routine.
- Expect individuals to refer to the event and discuss in the future.

6. ASSESSMENT
- Determine which students need further support.

GROUP DEBRIEFING

1. Ground Rules
- ▷ Confidentiality.
- ▷ No put downs, no interruptions.
- ▷ Speak for yourself.

2. Format
- ▷ Discuss facts/feelings.
- ▷ What did you see?
- ▷ What have you heard about the incident?
- ▷ What did you feel?

3. Identify Needs
- ▷ Sort out past and present events.

4. Reactions
- ▷ Watch for range of reactions.
- ▷ Note amusement about the incident, numbness, unaffected.

5. When It's Over
- ▷ Keep discussion focused until it goes its normal routine.
- ▷ Expect individuals to refer to incident in future.

6. Assessment
- ▷ Determine who needs support?

CLASSROOM DEBRIEFING

1. INTRODUCTION
The leader lays down the basic rules for participation.
- ▷ Introduction and purpose
- ▷ Confidentiality (what's said in here stays in here); no notes, taping, recording.
- ▷ No interrupting; No put-downs; Not here to blame anyone.
- ▷ Speak only for yourself. Pass if you do not want to speak.
- ▷ Everyone is equal here.

2. FACTS
Here students explore and gain concurrence on the sequence of events, and role each played in the incident.
- ▷ What happened?
- ▷ Who was involved?
- ▷ When it happened?
- ▷ Where it happened?
- ▷ How it happened?

3.THOUGHTS
- ▷ First thing you thought about.

4. REACTION
- ▷ Worst thing about incident.
- ▷ Your first reaction.
- ▷ How are you reacting now?
- ▷ What effect has this had on you?

5.SYMPTOMS
Each student is given the opportunity to share.
- ▷ What unusual things did you experience at the time?
- ▷ What unusual things are you experiencing now?
- ▷ Has your life changed in any way at home and school?

6.TEACHING
The leader provides information to the students regarding normal reactions to the incident, and anticipates later reactions. Any misconceptions regarding the incident or its effects can be cleared up.
- ▷ You are 100% normal if you have any of these **feelings**, **thoughts**, and **symptoms**.
- ▷ Denial, avoidance, sleep difficulties, irritability, fatigue, restlessness, depression/mood swings, difficulty concentrating, nightmares, vomiting/diarrhea, suspiciousness
- ▷ How have you coped with difficulties before?
- ▷ What are you doing to cope now?
- ▷ How will you know that things are getting better for you?

7. CLOSURE
- ▷ Remind students of strengths.
- ▷ Reassure them that it will take time to heal.
- ▷ Reassure them that you will be there.
- ▷ Any other questions?
- ▷ Want to add something?

INDIVIDUAL DEBRIEFING

1. FIND PRIVACY
Attempt to find a comfortable, private place for the conference. If the conference is to be individual, it must be private in order to engage trust. Avoid placing yourself in a compromising position, particularly if you are male with a female student. Stay visible to others.

2. MAINTAIN CALM
In all probability, the student is experiencing uncertainty and self-doubt. Presenting a balanced demeanor tells the student that what he/she is about to say will be accepted.

3. BE HONEST WITH YOURSELF
Keep in touch with your own feelings and reactions to the student, the issues, and the situation. If you feel you cannot handle the situations, ask someone else to take over, and arrange a transition.

4. READ BETWEEN THE LINES
Watch the student's behavior. Be aware of subtle messages. Draw inferences for further exploration.

5. VALIDATE FEELINGS
Feelings are neither right nor wrong. Whatever the feelings the student is experiencing, validate them by being present. Often lots of feelings clamor for expression; help the student clarify them, and you will both watch them change.

6. LISTEN WELL
Good listening involves several skills. Use gentle probes for clarification and elaboration. Maintain good eye contact. Use increasingly focused questions when appropriate (especially when you suspect harm). Trust your hunches, and check them out. (refer to section on empathic listening/questioning).

7. SHOW BELIEF
Your job at this point is to listen and to facilitate expression. You are not a judge, jury, or investigator. Show confidence, trust and faith that what the student is saying is the truth as he/she believes it to be.

8. DISPEL FAULT
If the student was victimized let him/her know that the incident was not their fault. Be proactive about this, because victims tend to distrust and blame themselves.

9. EXPLORE FEARS
Individuals often can tell about what happened to them, but may be unable to express assumptions they have made, questions they have, or fears they may hold about the incident. Facilitating the expression of these assumptions, questions, and fears at this point empowers the individuals to deal with them.

10. PROVIDE INFORMATION
The right information at the right time can be very helpful. If you know something about the incident, normal reactions to that type of incident, or actions that could be taken, consider sharing it; however, be sure not to preach and be sure that your own need to "do something" is not clouding your judgment regarding the timeliness of the information.

11. WALK THROUGH THE PROCESS
There are many processes, which are predictable, given a particular situation. Loss of a significant person will predictably involve the grief process. Disclosure of crime, victimization will predictably involve the police and other legal procedures. When the time is right, sharing what you know about certain procedures can assist the student in predicting and planning for their near future.

12. EXPLORE RESOURCES
As soon as possible, explore with the student what resources he/she has available, and what his/her support system provides. Assist him/her in deciding when, how, and to whom to reach out for that support.

OPERATIONAL DEBRIEFING

1. INTRODUCTION
- ▹ State purpose of the debriefing.
- ▹ State any ground rules.

2. FACTS OF THE INCIDENT
- ▹ Participants gain consensus on what happened.
- ▹ Participants gain consensus on the order things happened.
- ▹ The role of each team member.

3. ASSESSMENT OF THE INTERVENTION
- ▹ Review of team performance.
- ▹ Things done well.
- ▹ Areas for improvement.

4. REACTIONS
- ▹ Individual reaction during the incident.

5. INTERPRETATION OF RESPONSE
- ▹ Opportunity to make sense of the incident from a professional perspective.
- ▹ Chance to understand the incident.

6. PLANS FOR IMPROVEMENT
- ▹ Lessons learned for future crisis response.

7. CLOSING
- ▹ Plans to implement the lessons learned from the current incident.

SUICIDE RISK ASSESSMENT

1. Prior Suicidal Behavior?
- Previous attempts.
- Family history.

2. Current Suicide Plan?
- Specific plan.
- Access to lethal means.
- Has completed preparations.
- Has a specific time.

3. Resources, Internal and External?
- Low self-esteem & self-confidence.
- Negative outlook on life.
- Unrealistic goals and dreams.
- Poor physical & mental health.
- Few friends.
- Dysfunctional family.
- Poor role models to follow.
- No access to professional help.
- Unsatisfying job or academic career.

4. Take All Threats Seriously!
- The more points, the higher the risk.
- Investigate threats!

APPENDIX 3

Rapid Response Checklists

STOP!

IF A CRITICAL INCIDENT HAS OCCURRED GO TO THE *IMMEDIATE RESPONSE* BELOW THEN REFER TO THE MOST APPROPRIATE CRISIS, ASSESSMENT, OR INTERVENTION.

RAPID RESPONSE CHECKLISTS

IMMEDIATE RESPONSE

CRISIS

ASSESSMENTS

INTERVENTION

IMMEDIATE RESPONSE

Situation_____

Completed By_____Date_____

#		
1.	Immediately determined the seriousness of the situation.	☐
2.	Called 911 or other emergency number for help, ambulance, physician, police, or fire if necessary.	☐
3.	Got help for the victim and ensured the safety of everyone else.	☐
4.	Gathered facts and maintain confidentiality where necessary.	☐
5.	If a crime of violence was committed secured the scene and called police.	☐
6.	Notified families of the individuals involved in the situation.	☐
7.	Contacted the area superintendent.	☐
8.	Assembled school based crisis team and determined what to do.	☐
9.	Determined if extra support was needed from the Department.	☐
10.	Kept media out of the school; prepared a statement for release.	☐
11.	Kept unauthorized people away from the area.	☐
12.	Displayed relevant contact details on a notice board.	☐
13.	Assembled island crisis team and determined what to do.	☐
14.	Gathered facts and maintained confidentiality, where necessary.	☐
15.	Kept media out of the area; prepared a press release.	☐
16.	Kept unauthorized people away from the area.	☐

Adapted from Educational Service (1997)

IMMEDIATE RESPONSE – CONTACT INFORMATION

Agency/People	Contact	Number	Date
Police			
Fire			
Ambulance			
Social Worker			
Physician			
Clergy			
Parents/Guardian(s)			
Counselor			
Superintendent			
School Board Chair			
Band Office			
Poison Control			
Crisis Line			
School Bus Company			
Probation Officer			
School Psychologist			
School Council			
Tribal Leader/Chief			
Council			
Hospital			
Search & Rescue			
Aviation Authority			
Coast Guard			

SCHOOL/COMMUNITY CRISIS RESPONSE TEAM

School/Community:_____School Year:_____

Name	Responsibility	Phone (H)	Phone (O)
Alternate Members			

Post a copy of this form in the staff room.
Send a copy to your area Superintendent.
Retain a copy in school file.

TELEPHONE CONTACT TREE

Directions: Extend a chart like this far enough to fill in the names and telephone numbers for all school staff or community team members. Each person then has three people to call when he/she receives a call about a crisis. Distribute and post.

Name _____

\# _____

   Name _____

   \# _____

   Name _____

   \# _____

   Name _____

   \# _____

   Name _____

   \# _____

Name _____

\# _____

      Name _____

      \# _____

      Name _____

      \# _____

      Name _____

      \# _____

      Name _____

      \# _____

      Name _____

      \# _____

      Name _____

      \# _____

      Name _____

      \# _____

      Name _____

      \# _____

   Name _____

   \# _____

      Name _____

      \# _____

      Name _____

      \# _____

      Name _____

      \# _____

   Name _____

   \# _____

      Name _____

      \# _____

      Name _____

      \# _____

      Name _____

      \# _____

SUICIDE

Situation_____

Completed By_____**Date**_____

1.	**Acknowledged the suicide.** Did not try to hide or ignore it.	☐
2.	**Gathered crisis team together.** Determined what steps needed to be taken next.	☐
3.	**Informed all school staff.** Completed the Critical Incident Alert Form.	☐
4.	**Identified those students closest to victim.** These individuals will be affected the most by the suicide. Inform them of the suicide in private.	☐
5.	**Set up a student drop-in center in the library (secondary school only).** This will be used for students who are too upset to remain in class.	☐
6.	**Kept students in school.** It important not to have students leaving the school when they are emotionally upset unless they have been picked up by their parents.	☐
7.	**Remained visible and circulated throughout the school.** This is important during class changes and at lunch time.	☐
8.	**Kept newspaper and TV reporters out of the school.** All contacts with these should be with the principal or his/her designate.	☐
9.	**Prepared an information letter and sent to all parents.** Letter provides information that can help parents support their children during a crisis.	☐
10.	**Prepare a letter and to send to the victim's parents.**	☐
11.	**Provide coping strategies to those closest to the deceased to help them deal with the loss and to encourage them to seek help if they need it.**	☐

Adapter from Petersen, S., & Straub, R.L., (1992) & Educational Service (1997)

SUDDEN LOSS

Situation_____

Completed By_____**Date**_____

1.	**Acknowledged the loss and pain.**	☐
2.	**Told individuals about the signs and symptoms of acute traumatic stress and acute grief response.**	☐
3.	**Told students that counseling is available.**	☐
4.	**Provided the telephone number for the local crisis line.**	☐
5.	**Encouraged parents to help their children cope with the pain.** Be available and don't leave them alone.	☐
6.	**Tried to keep the stress down and avoided letting students form in large groups.** When students become emotionally upset they tend to feed off each other's emotionality and can be very difficult to handle.	☐
7.	**Provided the telephone number for any support services available.**	☐
8.	**Informed the public through the media of positive ways to express their feelings and how to cope with pain.**	☐
9.	**Provided emotional support and counseling where necessary for adults and children.**	☐
10.	**Avoided giving false information.**	☐

Adapted from Petersen, S. & Straub, R.L. (1992) & Educational Service (1997)

VIOLENCE

Situation_____

Completed By_____**Date**_____

1.	**Immediately went to the scene of the violence.** Do not run. Ask any students remaining in the area to leave.	☐
2.	**Did not attempt to take weapon away, if any involved.** Remain calm and call the police.	☐
3.	**Did not chase after any individuals who were running away from the scene.** Make a note as to whom, what, and where. Record as many details as you can.	☐
4.	**Conducted an informal assessment of the situation.**	☐
5.	**Contacted a doctor or called an ambulance if necessary.** Make sure that everyone else is safe.	☐
6.	**If a crime was committed, secured the area.** Attempt to preserve evidence.	☐
7.	**If necessary, called the police or security.**	☐
8.	**Secured the names of any witnesses and evidence of the crime.**	☐
9.	**Provided reassurance to the victim that he/she was safe.** You will protect them as best you can.	☐
10.	**Did not allow the victim and accused to come into contact.**	☐
11.	**Expressed to the victim and any witnesses the importance of reporting the incident.**	☐
12.	**Told the victim to report only the necessary details required.**	☐
13.	**Maintained the victim's privacy.**	☐
14.	**Had the victim consult with a lawyer.**	☐
15.	**If the victim was willing, had him/her examined by a doctor.** Important if the victim was sexually assaulted.	☐
16.	**If domestic violence, helped person report to the police.**	☐

Adapted from Petersen, S. & Straub, R.L. (1992) & Educational Service (1997)

LARGE SCALE DISASTER

Completed By   Date

1. Contacted government officials. ☐
2. Contacted the Atoll/Island/Tribal chiefs. ☐
3. Contacted Atoll/Island/Tribal task force. ☐
4. Established a hot line for information sharing. ☐
5. Contacted additional doctors. ☐
6. Contacted additional nurses. ☐
7. Identified people with special needs such as pregnant women, elderly, children, disabled. ☐
8. Are there volunteers to work? Are there people who can provide psychosocial support? ☐
9. Is there a safe water supply available? ☐
10. Determine who is responsible for providing accurate information to the public and affected people. ☐
11. Is there sufficient food available for the community and relief workers? ☐
12. Is there sufficient clothing for the community? ☐
13. Is evacuation necessary, if so, arranged transportation. ☐
14. Are there sufficient hygiene supplies (especially for women) available? ☐
15. Is there a need for temporary shelters or tents? ☐
16. Is there sufficient lighting available? ☐
17. Is there a place to take the injured? ☐
18. Is there a fear of disease outbreak? ☐
19. Are there sufficient medical supplies? ☐
20. Has a vaccination program started and for which diseases? ☐
21. Is there a place to store the dead and provide proper burial rites? ☐
22. Are people available to help store or bury the dead? ☐
23. Is transportation needed? Arranged transportation by sea/air/land. ☐
24. Is there an alternative means of communication available, mosque loud speakers school PA system? ☐

25. Is there sufficient security at temporary shelter 'camps'?   ☐

26. Is there shelter for the relief workers?   ☐

27. Have the relief workers been vaccinated?   ☐

28. Is the media there? Use the media to make public announcements about public health issues.   ☐

29. Is someone responsible for releasing information to the media?   ☐

30. Is there a need to make a team of volunteers to organize various tasks?   ☐

31. Are there donors for food and water?   ☐

32. If communications cut off, have arrangements been made for transportation to a location where information can be exchanged and gathered?   ☐

33. Has the Health Ministry been contacted?   ☐

34. Set up a crisis management task force.   ☐

35. Set up a shelter for foreign aid and supplies and managed it.   ☐

36. Make public announcements about the disaster.   ☐

Adapted from White & Peat, 2005.

MARINE DISASTER

Situation_____

Completed By_____Date_____

1. Clarified the seriousness of the situation.   □

2. Determined the location, water conditions, number of people
involved, and weather.   □

3. Called emergency numbers, coast guard, police,
or nearby resorts for help.   □

4. Identified possible alternatives to the coast guard
for immediate support.   □

5. Called island/atoll offices.   □

6. Called nearest hospital and health centers and made sure they are
prepared.   □

7. Made alternative arrangements for patients
if hospitals without enough room.   □

8. Assembled crisis team members.   □

9. Informed the families involved with individuals on the
vessel giving them contact numbers for updates and accurate information. □

10. Gathered facts and kept in contact with ferry terminal,
transportation ministry, police, & coast guard, for regular updates.   □

11. Arranged for or provided psychosocial support for victims   □

12. Contacted counselors, teachers, and other sources of support in the
community and prepared them to offer support.   □

13. Kept media away from those close to the victims and
prepared a news release.   □

Adapted from White & Peat, 2005.

INITIAL ASSESSMENT

Situation_____

Completed By_____ Date_____

1.	Will this situation affect the whole school community?	☐
2.	Might this situation get worse very quickly?	☐
3.	Might this situation recur?	☐
5.	Might this situation get out of control?	☐
6.	Is this situation susceptible to rumors and hysteria?	☐
7.	Is the event seen as important and threatening?	☐
8.	Is there evidence of strong emotional reaction?	☐
9.	Have normal coping behaviors been ineffective?	☐
10.	Is emotional discomfort increasing?	☐
11.	Is there evidence of repeated use of ineffective coping behaviors?	☐
12.	Is disorganization/psychological imbalance occurring?	☐
13.	Is turmoil increasing?	☐
14.	Has the School-based Crisis Team been activated?	☐
15.	Is assistance needed from the Divisional/Department crisis team?	☐
16.	Are rival gangs involved?	☐
17.	Is discipline or crowd control going to be a problem?	☐
18.	Did anyone witness the incident?	☐
19.	Located and spoke with individual(s) who witnessed the incident?	☐
20.	Are the witnesses traumatized?	☐
21.	Are there any groups that will be impacted? If so, who are they?	☐
22.	Are there any racial, cultural, or ethnic factors that may effect the situation?	☐
23.	Is the school safe for students?	☐
24.	Are staff members safe?	☐
25.	Are extra monitors required in classrooms?	☐
26.	Are some classes likely to be effected more than others?	☐
27.	Are there any staff members or adults who may be affected more than others?	☐
28.	Are there any legal issues that could affect operation of the crisis team?	☐
29.	Are some places/locations likely to be affected more than others?	☐
30.	Is there any fear that weapons are in the school?	☐
31.	Is there a need to call the police?	☐

Adapted from Fairchild, T.N. (1996) & Educational Service (1997)

INDIVIDUAL ASSESSMENT

Name_____

Completed By_____Date_____

MODERATE IMPAIRMENT DURING INCIDENT

1. The individual was confused. ☐
2. The individual had difficulty solving problems. ☐
3. The individual had difficulty prioritizing tasks. ☐
4. The individual exhibited time distortions. ☐
5. The individual exhibited sings of short-term memory loss. ☐
6. The individual exhibited signs of fear and anxiety. ☐
7. The individual exhibited signs of anger. ☐
8. The individual was irritable. ☐
9. The individual was easily frustrated. ☐
10. The individual complained of headaches. ☐
11. The individual complained of heart palpitations. ☐
12. The individual exhibited signs of muffled hearing. ☐
13. The individual complained of having nausea and cramps. ☐
14. The individual exhibited signs of rapid breathing. ☐
15. The individual was lethargic, wandering about aimlessly. ☐
16. The individual appeared to feel dejected. ☐

MODERATE IMPAIRMENT AFTER INCIDENT

1. The individual expressed fear of going crazy. ☐
2. The individual was preoccupied with the incident. ☐
3. The individual's orientation was constantly towards the past. ☐
4. The individual denied the importance of the incident. ☐
5. The individual had difficulty concentrating on tasks. ☐
6. The individual appeared to be depressed. ☐
7. The individual expressed guilt about the incident. ☐
8. The individual was afraid a similar incident would happen again. ☐
9. The individual had phobic reactions. ☐
10. The individual was suspected of having engaged in substance abuse. ☐
11. The individual exhibited signs of self-destructive behavior. ☐
12. The individual was withdrawn. ☐
13. The individual exhibited sudden changes in his/her life style. ☐

14.	The individual had difficulty sleeping.	☐
15.	The individual experienced flashbacks and nightmares.	☐
16.	The individual showed signs of clingy behavior, regressive behavior, bed wetting, thumb-sucking.	☐
17.	The individual experienced a loss of interest in daily activities.	☐
18.	The individual experienced difficulty making simple decisions.	☐
19.	The individual experienced difficulty making simple decisions.	☐
20.	The individual showed a loss of interest in pleasurable activities.	☐
21.	The individual experienced a change in appetite.	☐
22.	The individual experienced flashbacks and nightmares.	☐

SERIOUS IMPAIRMENT AFTER INCIDENT

1.	The individual could not tell name, date, or the event.	☐
2.	Exhibited signs of exclusive preoccupation with the event.	☐
3.	The individual denied that the event occurred.	☐
4.	The individual experienced hallucinations.	☐
5.	The individual experienced paralysis.	☐
6.	The individual was disconnected to his/her surroundings.	☐
7.	The individual acted on bizarre beliefs.	☐
8.	The individual was hysterical.	☐
9.	The individual threatened others.	☐
10.	The individual exhibited signs of physical shock.	☐
11.	The individual got into the fetal position.	☐
12.	The individual experienced panic attacks.	☐
13.	The individual exhibited signs of unfocused agitation.	☐
14.	The individual exhibited ritualistic acting out of the event.	☐
15.	The individual had difficulty caring for his/herself.	☐

Adapted from Johnson, K. (1993) & Educational Service (1997)

SUICIDE RISK ASSESSMENT

Name_____

Completed By_____Date_____

1.✔	Does the person have a specific plan?	☐
2.✔	Does the person have the means to carry out the plan?	☐
3.✔	Is the person prepared to commit suicide?	☐
4.✔	Has the person set a specific time to commit suicide?	☐
5.✔	Has the person tried to commit suicide before?	☐
6.✔	Is there a history of suicide in the person's family?	☐
7.✔	Does the person have low self-esteem?	☐
8.	Does the person have a negative outlook on life?	☐
9.	Does the person have unrealistic goals and dreams?	☐
10.✔	Does the person have poor physical health?	☐
11.✔	Does the person have poor mental health?	☐
12.✔	The person does not have friends and resources to talk with.	☐
13.✔	Does the person come from a dysfunctional family?	☐
14.	The person does not have a permanent home.	☐
15.	The person does not have access to professional help.	☐
16.	The person does not have positive role models to follow.	☐
17.✔	The person has started to make final arrangements.	☐
18.✔	The person has lost a significant friend etc. recently.	☐
19.	The person is withdrawn, has decreased social activity.	☐
20.	The person exhibits mood swings.	☐
21.	The person is taking unwarranted risks.	☐
22.	The person expresses self dislike, "I hate myself."	☐
23.	The person has a pattern of alcohol and drug abuse.	☐

Adapted from Ramsay, R., Tanney, B., Tierney, R., & Lang, W., (1994) & Educational Service (1997)

There are 13 significant indicators, (✔ Indicates significant factor).

Significant Indicators Marked:_____/13.

TEACHER'S ASSESSMENT

Situation_____

Completed By_____Date_____

1.	Read the information on the Critical Incident Alert form to the class.	☐
2.	Took a moment to share my feelings with the class.	☐
3.	Told the students about any changes in the classroom and school schedule.	☐
4.	Told the class that a notice about the memorial service would be announced as soon as it was available.	☐
5.	Told students not to contact the family of the deceased if seeking additional information.	☐
6.	Informed students that they would need permission from their parents to be excused from school to attend a funeral service.	☐
7.	Allowed time for any discussions that students wanted to have.	☐
8.	Wrote down questions that I could not answer and told students that I would get back to them later.	☐
9.	Told the class that if they heard any rumors, they should check them out with me.	☐
10.	Told students that some may expect to have trouble sleeping, eating, or concentrating.	☐
11.	Announced where the Student Drop-In Center is set up.	☐
12.	Asked the students to support each other.	☐
13.	Suspended any testing and reviews.	☐
14.	Maintained a relaxed structure and routine during the day.	☐
15.	Suggested concrete activities for students to work on.	☐
16.	Asked students how they were going to cope at home.	☐

Adapted from Educational Service (1997)

THREAT ASSESSMENT

1. School/Community:_____Date/Time:_____
____

2. Threat Maker:_____ ☐ Male   ☐ Female

3. Birth Date (M/D/Y):_____

4. Age:_____Grade:_____Teacher:_____

5. Home Address:_____

   Telephone:_____Home/Office:_____

6. Mother:_____Father:_____

7. Family Structure: ☐ Single Parent   ☐ Both Parents   ☐

   Foster Parents

                    ☐ Adopted   ☐ Grandparents   ☐ Siblings (Specify)
   _____

8. Threat Type: ☐ Traditional   ☐ Mixed Type   ☐ Nontraditional

9. Collaterals: ☐ No   ☐ Yes (Specify)_____
   _____
   _____

10. Target: ☐ Individual (Name)_____

            ☐ Multiple (Names)_____

            ☐ Object (Specify)_____

11. Type of Threat: ☐ Direct   ☐ Veiled   ☐ Indirect   ☐ Conditional

12. Delivery: ☐ Written   ☐ Verbal   ☐ Posted
            ☐ Drawing   ☐ Internet   ☐ Gesture

13. Threat Details:_____
   _____
   _____
   _____

_____
_____
_____

14. **Weapon Indicated:** ☐ No   ☐ Yes (Specify)   _____

_____
_____

____

15. **Time Frame:**   ☐ Morning   ☐ Afternoon   ☐ Night

16. **Specific Plan**   ☐ No   ☐ Yes (Specify)_____

_____
_____

____

17. **Police Contacted:** ☐ No   ☐ Yes (Specify Contact)_____

____

18. **Police Response:**_____

_____
_____

19. **Threat Assessment Team Assembled:**   ☐ Yes   ☐ No

20. **Team Members:**   A._____

                        B._____

                        C._____

                        D._____

                        E._____

                        F._____

                        G._____

21. **Risk Level:**   ☐ Immediate_____

_____
_____

☐ **Threat Making Behaviors (Specify)**_____

_____

_____

☐ **Worrisome Behaviors (Specify)**_____

_____

_____

☐ **High Profile Worrisome Behaviors (Specify)**_____

_____

_____

_____

22. **Threat Maker Interviewed:**   ☐ Yes   ☐ No

23. **Date:**_____**Time:**_____**Location:**_____

24. **How Much Time Do We Have:**_____

25. **Who Interviewed First:**_____

26. **Order of Interviewing and by Whom:**

      A._____

      B._____

      C._____

      D._____

      E._____

      F._____

      G._____

      H._____

      I._____

27. Observations (Check all that apply):

☐ Low Frustration Tolerance	☐ Externalizes Blame
☐ Poor Coping Skills	☐ Failed Love Relationship
☐ Signs of Depression	☐ Narcissism
☐ Dehumanizing Others	☐ Lacks Empathy
☐ Sense of Entitlement	☐ Attitude of Superiority
☐ Need for Attention	☐ Low Self-Esteem
☐ Anger Problem	☐ Intolerance
☐ Inappropriate Humor	☐ Manipulates Others
☐ Lack of Trust	☐ Closed Social Group
☐ Changed Behavior	☐ Rigid/Opinionated
☐ Interest in Violence	☐ Negative Role Models
☐ Likes Violent Entertainment	☐ Lacks Resiliency
☐ Conduct Problems	☐ Suspensions

28. Pre-Existing Conditions (Check all that apply):

☐ Oppositional Defiant	☐ ADHD
☐ Mood Disorder	☐ FASD
☐ Child Abuse	☐ Psychopathology
☐ Conduct Disorder	☐ Anxiety
☐ Depression	☐ Probation
☐ Suspension	☐ Other (Specify)_____

_____

_____

29.   Threat Assessment Report Completed: ☐ Yes   ☐ No

30.   Report Completed By:_____Date:_____

31.   Action Taken:_____

_____

_____

_____

_____

32.   Recommendations:_____

_____

_____

_____

33.   Follow-up:_____

_____

_____

_____

34.   Anniversary Date:_____

SUPPORT STRATEGIES

PRESCHOOLERS 3-6 YEARS /AFTER INCIDENT	
1. Limited their exposure to TV, books, papers about the incident.	☐
2. Encouraged them to draw pictures, make cards, write a letter.	☐
3. Answered questions calmly and limited scope.	☐
4. Spent extra time with children e.g., cooking, playing games.	☐
5. Reassured them that they are safe.	☐
6. Did not minimize the event.	☐
7. Did not lie or minimize own feelings.	☐
8. Did not make fun of regressive behaviors e.g. sucking thumb.	☐
9. Validated their feelings.	☐
10. Called the disaster by its name, not some other name.	☐
11. Reassured the child about the unusual nature of the event.	☐
12. Reassured the child that this recent event is gone.	☐

SCHOOL-AGED 6-12 YEARS /AFTER INCIDENT	
1. Limited their exposure to TV, books, papers about the incident.	☐
2. Held small group discussions and encouraged children to talk.	☐
3. Encouraged them to draw pictures, make cards, write a letter.	☐
4. Answered questions calmly and limited scope.	☐
5. Spent extra time with children, cooking, playing games.	☐
6. Kept a careful eye on kids who had previous problems	☐
7. Reassured them that they are safe.	☐
8. Did not minimize the event.	☐
9. Did not lie or minimize own feelings.	☐
10. Did not make fun of regressive behaviors e.g. sucking thumb.	☐
11. Validated their feelings.	☐
12. Called the disaster by its name, not some other name.	☐
13. Reassured the child about the unusual nature of the event.	☐
14. Reassured the child that this recent event is gone.	☐

ADOLESCENTS 12-18 YEARS /AFTER INCIDENT	
1. Limited their exposure to TV, books, papers about the incident.	☐
2. Encouraged them to draw pictures, make cards, write a letter.	☐
3. Answered questions calmly and limited scope.	☐
4. Spent extra time with children, cooking, playing games.	☐
5. Reassured them that they are safe.	☐
6. Did not minimize the event.	☐
7. Did not lie or minimize own feelings.	☐
8. Did not make fun of regressive behaviors e.g. sucking thumb.	☐
9. Validated their feelings.	☐
10. Called the disaster by its name, not some other name.	☐
11. Reassured the child about the unusual nature of the event.	☐
12. Reassured the child that this recent event is over.	☐
13. Held small groups to discuss the unusual nature of the crisis.	☐
14. Discussed the political, psychological, religious implications of the crisis.	☐
15. Did not allow scary or dramatic or inflammatory talk about crisis.	☐
16. Expected decline in individual work performance.	☐
17. Kept a special focus on children who were previously emotionally vulnerable or are currently experiencing emotionally difficulty.	☐
18. Watched for any signs of self-blame or self-criticism.	☐
19. Watched for any signs of increased irritability; if evident, explained the cause.	☐

Adapted from Jadis Blurton, Ph.D.

GROUP DEBRIEFING

Situation_____

Completed By_____**Date**_____

1.	Located private room to conduct group discussion in.	☐
2.	Stated ground rules.	
	(Confidentiality, no put-downs. Speak for yourself. No interruptions).	☐
3.	Asked each person what he/she heard.	☐
4.	Asked each person what he/she felt.	☐
5.	Asked each person when he/she heard about the incident.	☐
6.	Determined which individuals needed additional support.	☐
7.	Discussed individual reactions to the incident.	☐
8.	Identified individuals who needed ongoing counseling.	☐
9.	Kept the discussion focused and avoided tangents.	☐
10.	Gave counselor names of individuals needing ongoing counseling.	☐
11.	Contacted parents of individuals having difficulty coping.	☐
12.	Provided information about normal reactions to incident.	☐
13.	Provided information and included parents if they were at the school.	☐
14.	Kept everyone together for sometime. Try to keep the groups to about 15-20 individuals.	☐
15.	Encouraged the students to talk about the incident by asking direct and explicit questions. For example, "What was the worst part for you? Where were you when it happened?" Pay close attention to what you hear.	☐
16.	Prepared students and parents for reactions of:	

sleeplessness	lack of concentration	
nausea	crying	
irritability	demanding	
fear and anxiety	nightmares	
sweating	numbness	
withdrawing	clinging	☐

17.	Told students that the above reactions are normal.	☐
18.	Gave suggestions for coping with incident.	☐
19.	Told students that a follow-up will be provided.	☐

Adapted from Johnson, K. (1993) & Educational Service (1997)

CLASSROOM DEBRIEFING

Situation_____	**Room**_____
Completed By_____	**Date**_____

1.   Stated the ground rules before the debriefing started.

Parents are not invited into these sessions. No interruptions!

Each person speaks for him/her self.

You do not have to speak if you do not want to. No put-downs.

What is said in here is confidential   ☐

2.   Clearly stated the facts of the incident.

What happened? Who was involved in the incident?

Where were you when it occurred?

What role did you play in the incident?   ☐

3.   Asked questions to bring out feelings about the incident.

How did you first react when you heard the news?

What thoughts have you had? What ideas do you think about?

How are you reacting now? What effect has this had on you?   ☐

4.   Cleared up any misconceptions about the incident. Told students about possible reactions to the incident. Normalized their reactions.

Ask what symptoms they are experiencing now.

Ask how they have coped with difficulties before.

Ask what they are doing to cope now.

Ask what effect the incident has had on their life.

Explain the grief cycle.

Explain the signs and symptoms of Post Traumatic Syndrome.

Make sure that each individual has someone that he/she can talk to.   ☐

5.   Closed the session with a reminder of individual strengths and reassured them it would take time to heal. Reassured them that I/you would be there.   ☐

Adapted from Johnson, K. (1993) & Educational Service (1997)

INDIVIDUAL DEBRIEFING

Name_____

Completed By_____Date_____

1.	Had a private location in which to meet.	☐
2.	Remained calm when listening to the student.	☐
3.	Kept in touch with my own feelings and reactions to the student and incident.	☐
4.	Watched the student's behavior. Looked for hidden message.	☐
5.	Validated feelings. They are neither right nor wrong.	☐
6.	Listened well, maintained good eye contact and asked gentle, probing questions.	☐
7.	Showed belief and confidence in what the student told me. You are not a judge, jury, or investigator.	☐
8.	Dispelled fault. Did not let the student take the blame for the incident.	☐
9.	Explored individual fears associated with the incident.	☐
10.	Provided information about normal reactions.	☐
11.	Explained the grief process.	☐
12.	Determined if the individual has access to resources.	☐

Adapted from Johnson, K. (1993) & Educational Service (1997)

OPERATIONAL DEBRIEFING

Situation_____

Completed By_____**Date**_____

#		
1.	Clearly stated the purpose of the debriefing.	☐
2.	Stated the ground rules for the debriefing.	☐
3.	Restated the facts of the recent critical incident.	☐
4.	Ensured that team members gained consensus on what happened.	☐
5.	Ensured that team members gained consensus on the order in which things happened.	☐
6.	Restated the role and responsibility of each team member.	☐
7.	Reviewed overall team performance.	☐
8.	Determined which things were done well. Gained consensus from team members.	☐
9.	Determined areas that needed improvement. Gained consensus from team.	☐
10.	Determined individual reactions during the incident.	☐
11.	Ensured that each team member made sense of the incident from a professional perspective.	☐
12.	Ensure that each team member understood the incident and his/her response to it.	☐
13.	Determined what lessons the team had learned from the incident.	☐
14.	Determined what team changes needed to be made for future crisis response.	☐
15.	Developed a plan to implement the changes learned from the recent critical incident.	☐

Adapted from Johnson, K. (1993) & Educational Service (1997)

HANDLING THE MEDIA

Situation_____

Completed By_____**Date**_____

1.	**Developed a written statement.**	☐
2.	**Appointed spokesperson to speak with media.**	
	This should be the <u>Principal (or, if policy dictates, the communication officer)</u>.	☐
3.	**Kept all staff informed; watched for rumors.**	☐
4.	**Contacted press before they contacted school.** (Avoiding talking to the press will raise suspicions.)	☐
5.	**Set the time and location to meet with the press.**	
	It is important not to have the press wandering through the school.	☐
6.	**Set out restrictions for media while on school property.**	☐
7.	**Appointed a person to meet the press and take them to and from the meeting place.** Don't leave it to the press to wander to the meeting room unattended.	☐
8.	**Stressed positive action taken by the school in dealing with the incident.**	☐
9.	**Stressed services available to students.**	☐
10.	**Announced changes that had taken place after the incident had passed.**	☐
11.	**Clarified any misinformation with the media.**	☐

Adapted from Johnson, K. (1993) & Educational Service (1997)

CRISIS INFORMATION FORM

(To be completed without prejudice)

Adapted from Petersen, S., & Straub, R.L. (1992)

CONFIDENTIAL

Completed by:_____**Date:**_____

1. *Background Information*

Victim(s)	School/Community	Grade	Date Of Birth	Gender

2. *Family constellation (mother, father, sisters, brothers, others)*

_____

_____

_____

_____

_____

_____

3. *Incident facts (who, what, where, when, how, witnesses, others involved, relationships)*

_____

_____

_____

_____

_____

_____

_____

_____

_____

_____

4. *Contacts*

Contact	Position Notified	Contact Person	Date Time	Telephone Number
☐	Police			
☐	Parents/Guardian			
☐	Superintendent			
☐	Band Office			
☐	Social Worker			
☐	Nurse			
☐	Family Services			
☐	Mental Health			
☐	Tribal Chief			
☐	Council			
☐	Government Official			
☐	Other			

5. *Notes*

_____

_____

_____

_____

_____

_____

_____

_____

_____

_____

INITIAL CRISIS MANAGEMENT PLAN

(To be completed without prejudice)

Adapted from Petersen, S., & Straub, R.L. (1992)

Completed by:_____**Date:**_____

1. *Crisis Team*

Name	Telephone	Address

2. *Checking the Facts of the Crisis*

Police contact person:_____

Area Superintendent:_____

Other contact persons:_____

Coroner:_____
_____

3. *Incident facts (who, what, where, when, how, witnesses, others involved, relationships).*

_____

_____

_____

_____

_____

_____

_____

_____

_____

_____

4. *Announcing the Event to the School*

How will you tell the staff? _____

Place? _____

Time? _____

Method of Contact (include telephone tree)? _____

_____

Person presiding? _____

How will you announce the event to students? _____

Method of contact. _____

_____

_____

_____

Person(s) announcing? _____

Place? _____

Time? _____

Written announcement prepared: _____

_____

_____

_____

_____

_____

_____

_____

_____

_____

_____

_____

5. *Teachers' Responsibilities*

Check off what you want the teachers to do during the crisis

☐ Announce event in classroom.

☐ Identify students in need of counseling.

☐ Notify counselor of the number of students wanting counseling.

☐ Remove distraught students from the class and escort to counseling.

☐ Discuss the crisis (refer to suggestions).

☐ Postpone testing.

☐ Eliminate, shorten, and structure assignments for a few days.

☐ Involve class in constructive activities relating to the event (refer to suggestions).

☐ Discuss with students and prepare them for funeral attendance.

☐ Remove personal items from victim's desk.

6. *Counselor's Responsibilities*

☐ Inform feeder schools so they can provide support for affected students.

☐ Maintain a list of students counseled.

☐ Call parents of students counseled and provide suggestions as to how they can support their children who are very distressed

☐ Select and inform those students who should participate in the Memorial Service in either an active or advisory capacity.

☐ Set up and monitor student drop-in center.

☐ Conduct defusing sessions, group discussions, and debriefings.

Reschedule the following activities

_____

_____

_____

_____

_____

_____

Identify individuals who can work with students

name _____ phone # _____

name _____ phone # _____

name _____ phone # _____

name _____ phone # _____

name _____ phone # _____

7. *Principal's Responsibilities*

☐   Assign extra secretarial help for office or counselor (person & phone)

☐   Contact district personnel for support if needed.

☐   Stop notifications of student activity (scholarship reports, testing, placement, and attendance) from being sent to the home of a family whose child has died.

☐   Arrange for substitute teachers if needed.

☐   Contact area superintendent.

☐   Prepare information letter to send off to parents.

☐   Prepare media statement.

name _____ phone # _____

name _____ phone # _____

name _____ phone # _____

name _____ phone # _____

Rearrange seating, classes, programs, etc. as indicated by crisis. Changes to be made

_____

_____

_____

_____

Establish areas and locations for counseling and student drop-in center:

name _____ location _____

name _____ location _____

name _____   location _____

name _____   location _____

Keep staff updated _____

_____

_____

_____

Identify faculty and staff in need of counseling.

_____

_____

Emphasize facts and squelch rumors.

_____

_____

Remain highly visible.

_____

_____

Arrange for excused absences and transportation for students attending off-premises funeral.

_____

_____

Arrange for staff debriefing.

Where? _____

When? _____

Who will preside? _____

Contact parents of students who have died _____

_____

8. *Handling the Media*

Spokesperson appointed

Alternate appointed

Person appointed to escort media

People to handle the telephone

Message to be given over the telephone

Media Release developed (complete Media Information Release Form).

Establish time and location to meet media

Identify person to speak to concerned parents

9. *Memorial Service*

Is a memorial service indicated in this crisis?

How many students will be attending?

Location?

Presiding person?

Speakers? _____

Coordinator _____

Student involvement (student names and roles) _____

_____

_____

_____

Activities _____

_____

_____

_____

_____

_____

Area for staff and students not wishing to participate _____

_____

_____

Community people who should be invited _____

_____

_____

10. *Adapting the Plan to Fit the Crisis*

_____

_____

_____

_____

_____

DAY-ONE OPERATIONAL CHECKLIST

Directions: Below are 48 items to monitor when developing an operational plan for the first day after a critical incident.

Completed By:_____**Date:**_____

1. ☐ Verified information and checked the facts of the incident with police.
2. ☐ Contacted the area Superintendent.
3. ☐ Completed the **Crisis Information Form** and sent it to area superintendent.
4. ☐ Met with all teaching and support staff to announce crisis before school started.
5. ☐ Met with the School Crisis Intervention Team before school started.
6. ☐ Identified high risk individuals and relatives closest to the victim.
7. ☐ Contacted feeder schools.
8. ☐ Developed a list of staff whom may need support in the classroom.
9. ☐ Determined if School Based Crisis Team can handle critical incident.
10. ☐ Established a central control point for entry to and exit from the school.
11. ☐ Set up a sign in/out log for students picked up/dropped off by parents.
12. ☐ Set up a telephone log to track all inquiries about the incident.
13. ☐ Developed approved information statement to be given out over telephone.
14. ☐ Clearly stated procedure for handling requests or call from parents and media.
15. ☐ Assigned staff person to retrieve students if parents want to remove them from school.
16. ☐ Requested help from counselors at feeder schools with debriefing activities.
17. ☐ Brought in extra support staff for the front office.
18. ☐ Brought in substitute teachers familiar with the school and students to provide support in classrooms requesting such.
19. ☐ Set up a Student Drop-In Center (secondary schools only).
20. ☐ Set up rotation schedule for staff working in Student Drop-In Center.
21. ☐ Set up counseling areas and assigned staff.
22. ☐ Assigned hall and washroom monitors to keep students from wandering.
23. ☐ Assigned roles and responsibilities to all staff.
24. ☐ Commenced Defusing Emotions sessions.
25. ☐ Assigned debriefing teams and started classroom debriefings.
26. ☐ Developed a list of students absent.
27. ☐ Developed a list of students who attended counseling.
28. ☐ Developed a list of students who required further counseling.
29. ☐ Contacted all parents of any students having difficulty coping.
30. ☐ Developed a list of staff persons absent.

31. ☐ Developed a list of staff that may need counseling.

32. ☐ Assigned staff person to remove victim's personal effects from locker.

33. ☐ Prepared a statement for the media regarding the response at the school.

34. ☐ Contacted the media and arranged time and location for meeting.

35. ☐ Assigned a staff person to escort media to and from the front door before and after the meeting.

36. ☐ Scheduled a follow-up meeting time and location with media.

37. ☐ Prepared information letter to parents to be sent home with all students.

38. ☐ Contacted the school bus company about incident and cautioned about possible changes in student's behavior.

39. ☐ Instructed teachers to postpone testing and have lower expectations for students.

40. ☐ Established a waiting area for parents who come to the school.

41. ☐ Assigned front office staff to escort parents to waiting area.

42. ☐ Ensured that there were light refreshments in the parent waiting area.

43. ☐ Informed school council that the crisis plan had been implemented.

44. ☐ Ensured ongoing contact and support for caregivers.

45. ☐ Scheduled breaks for all staff.

46. ☐ Met with all staff after to school to up date.

47. ☐ Met with School Crisis Team after school to re-evaluate plan.

48. ☐ Scheduled staff debriefing date for all teaching and support staff.

49. ☐ Other_____

50. ☐ Other_____

51. ☐ Other_____

52. ☐ Other_____

53. ☐ Other_____

54. ☐ Other_____

55. ☐ Other_____

DAY-TWO OPERATIONAL CHECKLIST

Directions: Below are 23 items to monitor when developing an operational plan for the second day after a critical incident.

Completed By:_____**Date:**_____

1. ☐ Met with all staff and up dated before school started.

2. ☐ Met with the School Crisis Team before school started and re-evaluated plan.

3. ☐ Maintained Student Drop-In Center.

4. ☐ Continued to provide classroom support for teachers requesting it.

5. ☐ Continued to have staff person monitor hallways and washrooms.

6. ☐ Maintained telephone log.

7. ☐ Maintained sign in/out log for students leaving the school.

8. ☐ Continued defusing sessions.

9. ☐ Continued classroom debriefing sessions.

10. ☐ Continued student counseling sessions.

11. ☐ Maintained central entry and exit to and from the school.

12. ☐ Continued to maintain a list of students who attended counseling.

13. ☐ Continued to keep extra front office staff.

14. ☐ Maintained the parent reception area.

15. ☐ Continued to have a front office staff person escort parents to reception area.

16. ☐ Continued to provide light refreshments in parent area.

17. ☐ Continued to provide light refreshments for staff and support workers.

18. ☐ Contacted parents of the victim and determined their wishes about disposition of personal affects and response by school and students.

19. ☐ Determined which students wanted to attend the funeral.

20. ☐ Ensured that students attending the funeral had been prepared for what to expect.

21. ☐ Met with all staff after school to up date.

22. ☐ Met with School Crisis Team after school to re-evaluate plan.

23. ☐ Scheduled staff debriefing for after school.

24. ☐ Other_____

25. ☐ Other_____

26. ☐ Other_____

27. ☐ Other_____

DAY-THREE OPERATIONAL CHECKLIST

> **Directions:** Below are 12 items to monitor when developing an operational plan for the third day after a critical incident.

Completed By:_____**Date:**_____

1. ☐ Met with all school staff before school started and up dated.

2. ☐ Met with School Crisis Team before school started and re-evaluated response plan.

3. ☐ Assigned staff person to clear out victim's desk.

4. ☐ Saved victim's personal belonging for parents.

5. ☐ Discussed with staff plans for a school memorial service.

6. ☐ Identified students who wanted to attend the memorial service.

7. ☐ Met with counselor(s) and determined which students needed further assistance.

8. ☐ Instructed teaching staff to resume more structure and routine in class.

9. ☐ Scheduled a follow-up meeting with school staff to occur two weeks after the incident.

10. ☐ Re-evaluated response to determine if there were any points not dealt with.

11. ☐ Maintained student drop-in center.

12. ☐ Compiled a list of students wishing to attend the funeral (parental permission required).

13. ☐ Other_____

14. ☐ Other_____

15. ☐ Other_____

16. ☐ Other_____

17. ☐ Other_____

18. ☐ Other_____

19. ☐ Other_____

20. ☐ Other_____

TELEPHONE LOG

School:_____Sheet Number:_____

Start Date:_____   End Date:_____

Date Time	Name Number	Inquiry	Follow-Up
			☐
			☐
			☐
			☐
			☐
			☐
			☐
			☐
			☐
			☐
			☐
			☐
			☐
			☐
			☐
			☐
			☐
			☐
			☐

CRITICAL INCIDENT ALERT FORM

Date:_____ **Time:**_____

To:_____

From:_____

School/Community:_____

Subject:_____

Verified Factual Information:

*When:*_____

_____

_____

*Who:*_____

_____

_____

_____

*Where:*_____

_____

_____

_____

_____

*How:*_____

_____

_____

_____

_____

_____

CLASSROOM SUPPORT REQUEST LOG

School:_____**Sheet Number:**_____

Start Date:_____   **End Date:**_____

Room #	Teacher	Person Assigned	Duration

STUDENT SIGN OUT LOG

School:_____**Sheet Number:**_____

Start Date:_____   **End Date:**_____

Date Time	Name	Parent Contact	Picked Up
		☐	☐
		☐	☐
		☐	☐
		☐	☐
		☐	☐
		☐	☐
		☐	☐
		☐	☐
		☐	☐
		☐	☐
		☐	☐
		☐	☐
		☐	☐
		☐	☐
		☐	☐
		☐	☐
		☐	☐
		☐	☐
		☐	☐

SCHOOL VISITORS LOG

School:_____**Sheet Number:**_____

Start Date:_____   **End Date:**_____

Date Time	Initial	Name	Purpose

CRITICAL INCIDENT INTERVENTION REQUEST

1. Request Date/Time:_____/_____ Report Number:_____

2. Requested By:_____Position:_____

3. School:_____

4. Location:_____

5. Office Telephone:_____Home Telephone:_____

6. Request Issued To:_____Position:_____

7. Department/Unit:_____

8. Office Telephone:_____Home Telephone:_____

9. Summary of Incident:_____

_____

_____

_____

_____

10. Date of Incident:_____Time:_____

11. **Urgency of Request:**

☐ **Immediate response**   ☐ **Response within 48 hours**

☐ **Response within 7 hours**   ☐ **Response within five days**

☐ **Response within 24 hours**   ☐ **Follow-up within two weeks**

12. **Total Participants:**

Staff:_____Students:_____Grade Levels:_____

13. **Intervention(s) Requested:**

☐ **Defusing Sessions**   ☐ **Individual Counseling**

☐ **Classroom Debriefings**   ☐ **Operational Debriefing**

☐ **Individual Debriefings**   ☐ **General Support**

☐ **Group Discussions**   ☐ **First Nations Consultant**

☐ **Follow-Up**   **Other (specify):**_____

14. **Active School Crisis Team:**   Yes ☐   No ☐

15. **School Crisis Team Member(s):**

1_____   3_____

2_____   4_____

16. **School Team Leader:**_____**Contact Number:**_____

17. **Additional Information/Instructions:**_____

_____

_____

Signature:_____Date:_____

EXTERNAL SUPPORT REQUEST RECORD

School/Community:_____**Date:**_____

Requested by:_____**Position:**_____

Directions: Below are a number of sources that may be contacted to provide additional support to the School Based Crisis Response Team during a critical incident. Check off each source that has been contacted and whether those sources have responded.

SUPPORT REQUESTED

Name/Number

☐   Superintendent or Designate.   _____/_____

☐   School Psychologist   _____/_____

☐   Family and Children's Services.   _____/_____

☐   Social Services.   _____/_____

☐   Youth probation.   _____/_____

☐   Mental Health Services.   _____/_____

☐   First Nations Consultant.   _____/_____

☐   Substitute teachers.   _____/_____

☐   Secretarial assistance   _____/_____

☐   Custodial assistance   _____/_____

☐   Medical assistance   _____/_____

☐   Nursing assistance   _____/_____

☐   School counselors   _____/_____

☐   Emergency specialists   _____/_____

☐   Police   _____/_____

☐   School Council.   _____/_____

☐   Parental support.   _____/_____

☐   Financial assistance.   _____/_____

☐   Maintenance   _____/_____

☐   Other (specify)   _____/_____

☐   Other (specify)   _____/_____

☐   Other (specify)   _____/_____

☐   Other (specify)   _____/_____

☐   Other (specify)   _____/_____

REFERRAL FOR COUNSELING

School:_____ Sheet Number:_____

Start Date:_____   End Date:_____

Date Time	Name	Risk Level	Parent Contact
			☐
			☐
			☐
			☐
			☐
			☐
			☐
			☐
			☐
			☐
			☐
			☐
			☐
			☐
			☐
			☐
			☐
			☐
			☐

LEVEL OF RISK   **1**/ Low **2**/Moderate **3**/High

SUICIDE PREVENTION CONTRACT

I,_____, agree that I will not attempt to committee suicide

or hurt myself in any way for the next _____ days. If I feel that I will try to break this

contract I will contact _____ at _____

immediately if I am at school. If I am not at school I will contact

_____ at _____ immediately.

I agree that I will not make any final decision or attempt at committing suicide until I

have talked with my counselor/helper directly.

This contract is effective immediately.

_____   _____

Student   Date

_____   _____

Counselor   Date

CLASSROOM ANNOUNCEMENT FORM

Directions: Please read this information to your class. If you do not feel comfortable presenting this, request assistance.

*When:*_____

*Who:*_____

*Where:*_____

*How:*_____

*Student Resources:*_____

_____

*Student Drop-In Center:*_____

☐　　　Read notice to class.

☐　　　Conduct classroom debriefing session, defusing, and group discussions.

☐　　　Allow students to attend student drop-in center (secondary school).

☐　　　Request classroom support if needed.

☐　　　Request crisis team member read notice if unable to do so.

☐　　　Suspend any student testing.

☐　　　Reduce student workload.

☐　　　Refer students for counseling if needed.

☐　　　Continue to maintain minimum structure and routine.

☐　　　Do not allow students to roam the halls.

☐　　　Identify students at risk.

☐　　　Take time for yourself.

NOTE: Simplify the above information when debriefing lower elementary grades.

MEDIA INFORMATION RELEASE

DO NOT STATE VICTIM(S) NAME (unless parent permission given).CLARIFY MISINFORMATION.

School/Community:_____**Date:**_____

Location:_____**Time:**_____

School Spokesperson:_____

Media Representatives:_____

Media Restrictions:

☐   **Access limited to meeting room only.**
☐   **Wandering about the school prohibited.**
☐   **Student interviews prohibited while on school property.**
☐   **Staff interviews prohibited unless approved by Principal.**
☐   **Photography while on school property prohibited.**
☐   **Other**_____

*When:*_____

_____

*Who:*_____

_____

*Where:*_____

_____

*How:*_____

_____

*Positive Action Taken:*_____

_____

*Changes Made After Incident:*_____

_____

*Services Available to Students:*_____

Follow Up Meeting Scheduled: YES☐   NO☐

*Location:*_____*Date:*_____*Time:*_____

MEMORIAL SERVICE RECORD

School/Community:_____**Location:**_____

Service Date/Time:_____/_____**Location:**_____

Service Organizer:_____**Contact Number:**_____

Total Students/Staff Attending:_____/_____

Parents Attending: Yes ☐   No ☐

Transportation Required: Yes ☐   No ☐

Seating Arranged: Yes ☐   No ☐

Officiating Clergy:_____**Contact Number:**_____

Officiating Clergy:_____**Contact Number:**_____

Guest Speakers:

1_____2_____

Student Speakers:

1_____2_____

Music Selections/Hymns:

1_____2_____

3_____4_____

Readings:

1_____2_____

3_____4_____

Floral Arrangements: Yes ☐   No ☐

Reception Area Prepared: Yes ☐   No ☐

Refreshments Available: Yes ☐   No ☐

Student Tributes: Yes ☐   No ☐

Community Guests Invited: Yes ☐   No ☐

1_____2_____

3_____4_____

Specific Religious Concerns/Instructions:_____

_____

_____

_____

_____

Waiting Area for Staff/Students Not Participating: Yes ☐   No ☐

Location:_____

SCHOOL/COMMUNITY CRITICAL INCIDENT PLAN REVIEW

Directions: Indicate which part(s) and/or procedure(s) of your school critical incident plan have been reviewed, revised, amended, or deleted.

School/Community:_____**Date:**_____

Action Taken By:_____**Position:**_____

Start Date:_____   **Close Date:**_____

Initial Response
☐   Reviewed (specify):_____

☐   Revised (specify):_____

☐   Amended (specify):_____

☐   Deleted (specify):_____

Day One Plan
☐   Reviewed (specify):_____

☐   Revised (specify):_____

☐   Amended (specify):_____

☐   Deleted (specify):_____

Day Two Plan
☐   Reviewed (specify):_____

☐   Revised (specify):_____

☐   Amended (specify):_____

☐   Deleted (specify):_____

Day Three Plan
☐   Reviewed (specify):_____

☐   Revised (specify):_____

☐   Amended (specify):_____

☐   Deleted (specify):_____

Forms
☐   Forms reviewed (specify):_____

☐   Forms revised (specify):_____

☐   Amended (specify):_____

☐   Deleted (specify):_____

Follow-up
☐   Reviewed (specify):_____

☐   Revised (specify):_____

☐   Amended (specify):_____

☐   Deleted (specify):_____

Staff Training

- ☐   Reviewed (specify):_____
- ☐   Revised (specify):_____
- ☐   Amended (specify):_____
- ☐   Deleted (specify):_____

FOLLOW-UP CHECKLIST

Completed By:_____   **Date:**_____

---

1. ☐ Recorded the anniversary date of the incident for future reference.
2. ☐ Determined if the counselor saw all students identified at risk.
3. ☐ Ensured that parents of all students at risk were contacted.
4. ☐ Ensured that all school staff attended a debriefing session within the first week.
5. ☐ Ensured that the school based crisis team attended an operational debriefing session within two weeks after the incident.
6. ☐ Scheduled a follow-up session with staff to occur six weeks after the incident.
7. ☐ Sent out personal thank you notes to all substitutes teachers, counselors, parent, and organizations that helped in some way during the critical incident.
8. ☐ Other (specify)_____
9. ☐ Other (specify)_____
10. ☐ Other (specify)_____
11. ☐ Other (specify)_____
12. ☐ Other (specify)_____

CRITICAL INCIDENT REPORT

1. **Report Date:**_____**Report Number:**_____

2. **Response Start Date/Time:**_____/_____

3. **Response Close Date/Time:**_____/_____

4. **Total Response Time: (Days)**_____**(Hours)**_____

5. **School/Community Initiated Request:**   Yes ☐   No ☐

6. **District/Department Initiative:**   Yes ☐   No ☐

7. **School/Community:**_____

8. **Location:**_____

9. **Principal/Official:**_____**Contact Number:**_____

10. **District/Department Team Dispatched By:**_____

11. **Position:**_____**Contact Number:**_____

12. **Summary of Incident:**

    Date:_____**Time:**_____

    Who:_____

    Where:_____

    What:_____

    How:_____

13. **Victim(s):**

    Ethnicity: C/Caucasian B/Black FN/First Nations IN/Inuit A/Asian I/Indian O/Other

    Status: D=Deceased I=Injured

    Cause: 1=Suicide 2=Accident 3=Homicide 4=Natural 5=Illness 6=Sudden Loss

Name	*Age*	*Grade*	*Ethnic*	*Status*	*Cause*
1_____	/	/	/	/	/
2_____	/	/	/	/	/
3_____	/	/	/	/	/
4_____	/	/	/	/	/

14. **Sibling(s)/Witnesses:**   Yes ☐   No ☐

Name	*Age*	*Grade*
1_____	/	/
2_____	/	/
3_____	/	/
4_____	/	/

15. **Total Deceased:**_____**Total Injured:**_____

16. **Total Student Population:**_____**Total Staff:**_____

17. **Total Number of Grades:**_____

18. **School Crisis Team Participation:**   Yes ☐   No ☐

19. District/Department Crisis Team Participation: Yes ☐   No ☐

20. External Agency(s) Involved: Yes ☐   No ☐

     Contact   *Number*

    1_____ / _____

    2_____ / _____

    3_____ / _____

    4_____ / _____

21. Intervention(s) Requested:

☐ Defusing Sessions   ☐ Individual Counseling

☐ Classroom Debriefings   ☐ Operational Debriefing

☐ Individual Debriefings   ☐ General Support

☐ Group Discussions   ☐ First Nations Consultant

☐ Follow-Up   ☐ Other (specify):_____

22. District/Department Team Members: **School Crisis Team Members:**

   1 (Leader)_____   1 (Leader)_____

   2_____   2_____

   3_____   3_____

   4_____   4_____

   5_____   5_____

   6_____   6_____

23. School Memorial Service Held: Yes ☐   No ☐

24. Memorial Service Date/Time:_____ / _____

_____

25. At Risk Students Identified: Yes ☐   No ☐

26. Parent(s)/Guardian Contacted: Yes ☐   No ☐

27. Follow-Up Date(s):

   1_____

   2_____

28. Recommendations:

   1_____

   2_____

   3_____

   4_____

Signature:_____

Date:_____

Witness:_____

CRITICAL INCIDENT LOG

Sheet Number:_____

Start Date:_____**Close Date:**_____

Date Report	School Incident	Students Staff	Injury Death	Age Grade	Cause Ethnic.	Time Action

CAUSE S/Suicide A/Accident H/Homicide N/Natural I/Illness SL/Sudden Loss
ETHNICITY C/Caucasian FN/First Nations B/Black O/Oriental G/German I/Indian OR/Other
ACTION 1/Defusing 2/Group Discussion 3/Individual Debriefing 4/Classroom Debriefing
5/counselling 6/General Support 7/First Nations Consultant 8/Oerational Debriefing 9/Follow-Up
10/Other
TIME Time spent at the school expressed in hours and/or days.

ISBN 142516579-6

9 781425 165796